SOUTH

the **race** to the Pole

'Scott for scientific method,
Amundsen for speed and efficiency
but when disaster strikes and all hope is gone,
get down on your knees and pray for Shackleton.'

Raymond Priestley, civilian geologist and meteorologist,
Nimrod and *Terra Nova* expeditions.

First published in 2000 by the National Maritime Museum, Greenwich, London, SE10 9NF.

ISBN: 0 948065 37 0

Designed by Bernard Friedman

Printed and bound in the UK by Cambridge University Press.

Acknowledgements:

John Shears, British Antarctic Survey; Kåre Berg, Director, Fram Museum, Oslo; Jacqui McLeod; Jane Ace, Tina Chambers, Harvey Edser, Ken Hickey, Alasdair Macleod, Rob Petherick, National Maritime Museum; Ann Savours (Shirley), polar expert and former Keeper of Manuscripts, National Maritime Museum; Per Olav Torgnesskar, Assistant Curator, National Library of Norway, Oslo Division, Picture Collection; Gerard A. Sellek, Department of Chemical Engineering, University of Bath; Max Jones, University of Cambridge; Philippa Smith, Scott Polar Research Institute, University of Cambridge; Elizabeth Wiggans, Indexer; David E. Yelverton, Fellow of the Royal Geographical Society; Linda Zealey, Foreign and Commonwealth Office, London.

Credits

Images are listed by page number. © The British Library, 79 (bottom); Reproduced by kind permission, Fram Museum, Norway (images © NMM), 57 (bottom), 58, 59, 60, 72, 87 (bottom), 89 (right), 90, 101; © Hulton Getty Picture Collection: 91; © Mirror Syndication International: 51(right), 53; © National Library of Norway, Oslo Division, Picture Collection: 19 (top), 57 (top), 67 (top), 74, 81 (bottom), 89 (left); © National Maritime Museum: 2, 9, 14, 15, 16, 17, 19 (bottom), 23, 36, 44, 47, 49, 50, 55, 62, 64, 65, 66, 67 (bottom), 69, 73 (top), 75 (bottom), 81 (top), 96, 112, 129; © Science Photo Library: 80; © Scott Polar Research Institute, University of Cambridge: cover, 10, 11, 12, 13, 20, 21, 22, 24, 25, 26, 27, 28, 29, 30, 31, 33, 34, 38, 39, 40/41, 42, 43, 48, 51 (left), 52, 63, 68, 70, 73 (bottom), 75, 76, 77, 78/79, 82, 85, 87 (top), 92, 93, 94, 95, 97, 98, 99, 102, 104, 105, 107, 109, 110, 111, 113, 114, 115, 116, 117, 118, 119, 121, 122, 123, 127, 128, 130, 133 (top); © Gerard A. Sellek: 133 (bottom). *Food for the Race to the Pole* (Chapter 5) is based on material from Robert E. Feeney's *Polar Journeys. The Role of Food and Nutrition in Early Expeditions* (Fairbanks: © University of Alaska Press and American Chemical Society, 1997) reprinted by kind permission of the publishers. Extracts from: R.F. *The Voyage of the Discovery* (London, John Murray Publishers, Ltd., 1905); L. Huxley, *Scott's Last Expedition*, Volumes 1 and 2 (London, John Murray Publishers, Ltd., 1913); A. Cherry-Garrard *The Worst Journey in the World* (London: Chatto and Windus Ltd., 1922); R. Amundsen *The South Pole* Vol. 1 (London: John Murray Publishers, Ltd., 1913).
(While every effort has been made to contact and obtain permission from holders of copyright, if any involuntary infringement of copyright has occurred, sincere apologies are offered.)

Cover picture:
30 October 1902. Photograph taken by Louis Bernacchi on the British National Antarctic Expedition, 1901-04, showing Michael Barne's Southern Support Party setting out.

Half-title recto:
Scott's sledging flag, British Antarctic Expedition, 1910-13. (33cm x 84cm, 13ins x 33ins)

SOUTH

the **race** to the Pole

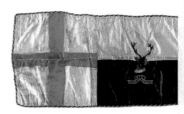

WORCESTERSHIRE COUNTY COUNCIL	
230	
Cypher	20.10.02
919.89	£14.99

Sponsored by:

A T Kearney Ltd

Supported by:

Burberry Ltd
Canadian Pacific
The Corporation of Trinity House
Orient Lines

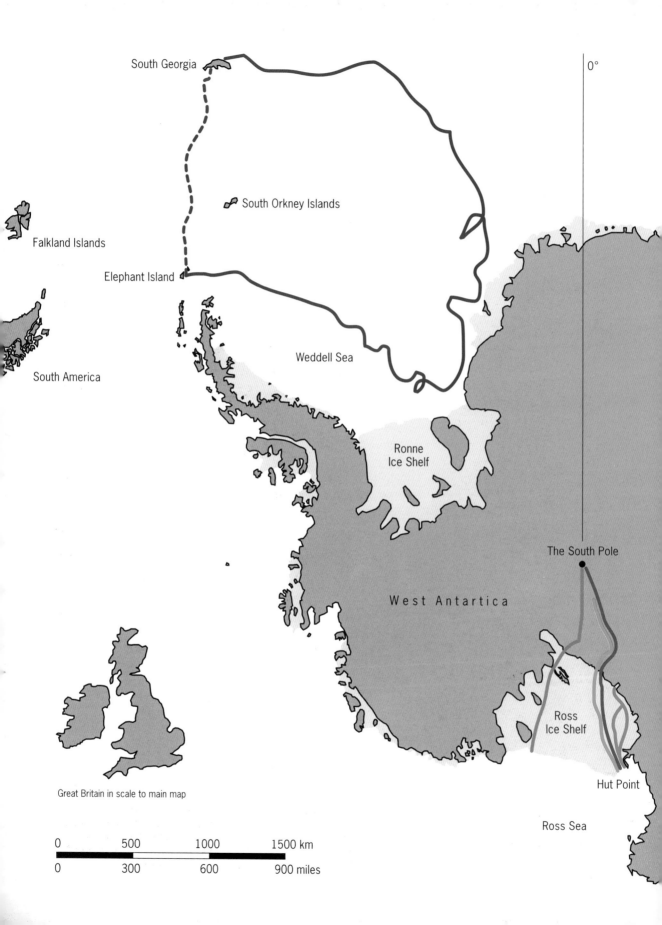

South Georgia

Falkland Islands

Elephant Island

South America

South Orkney Islands

Weddell Sea

Ronne
Ice Shelf

West Antartica

The South Pole

0°

Ross
Ice Shelf

Hut Point

Ross Sea

Great Britain in scale to main map

0	500	1000	1500 km
0	300	600	900 miles

Contents

East Antartica

———— *Discovery* 1901–04
———— *Nimrod* 1907–09
———— *Fram* 1910–12
———— *Terra Nova* 1910–13
———— *Endurance* 1914–17

Figures quoted for the overall length of polar journeys vary. In this account approximate overall lengths are given in statute miles (5,280ft/1.6km) for general comprehension with nautical or geographical mile equivalents (6,080ft/1.85km) where appropriate. Intermediate distances are, following sources used, generally in nautical miles (60nm = 1 degree of latitude = 69.05 statute miles).

Foreword

As a participant in the first Whitbread round-the-world yacht race in 1973, I sampled a little of the excitement and the fright that go with the drive to probe the boundaries of our existence. Sailors, aviators, divers and mountaineers are among countless millions of us who, within our physical capabilities, take on various dimensions of the planet's environment each weekend.

In this fashion, we amateurs hardly ever create legends, but our pulses race and our personal conquests help to define the much greater achievements of others. Stimulated by primeval instincts to explore, to compete and to survive, mankind thrives on such adventures, even if our individual challenges are puny, bounded by the limits of our stamina and courage.

Indeed, our collective efforts are as specks of dust alongside this monumental story. *South: the race to the Pole* is the first major exhibition on Antarctic exploration to be presented by the National Maritime Museum. Supported by this book, it describes an international race to an invisible and profitless point, in the middle of the most unexplored, climatically hostile continent on earth.

The focus is on those who ran the last laps of that race: Roald Amundsen, who won; Robert Falcon Scott, who lost and died; and Ernest Shackleton, who turned Antarctic failure into personal triumph, even as the age of European empire – whose rivalries fuelled the competition – was consumed by World War I.

Within these pages the stirring enterprise is placed in geographical and historical context, while the exhibition features objects, photographs and film that survived the terrible conditions those brave men endured, and which still bear witness to the legends they created in that 'heroic age' of pre-war Antarctic discovery.

On behalf of everyone at the Museum I have the privilege and pleasure to welcome you, our visitors, to this exciting new presentation at Greenwich. I hope you enjoy both this book and the exhibition and that you may take the opportunity to visit our website (www.nmm.ac.uk).

I would also like to thank the many public institutions and private collectors who have lent items for the exhibition, selections of which are illustrated in these pages. We are particularly indebted to the Fram

Museum in Oslo, whose generous co-operation has enabled the part of Roald Amundsen to be shown so well; to the Scott Polar Research Institute, Cambridge; and to the Royal Geographical Society. We are also most grateful to AT Kearney Ltd, the Corporation of Trinity House, Orient Lines and Burberry Ltd for their financial support.

Finally, as the incoming Director of the Museum, I would like to thank all who have helped prepare *South: the Race to the Pole,* especially the staff team at Greenwich. Among the latter, Sian Flynn has worked tirelessly in researching the exhibition and Pieter van der Merwe no less so as principal author of the book. Our thanks also go to its external contributors: Diana Preston, Robert E. Feeney and Luke McKernan.

This is the last exhibition completed under my distinguished predecessor, Richard Ormond; it is also the first major display in the Canadian Pacific Special Exhibitions Gallery of the new Museum, so successfully redeveloped under his hand. He has set high standards for me to follow and I am delighted to have this early opportunity to pay public tribute to his very significant achievements as Director since 1986.

Roy Clare
Director
National Maritime Museum, Greenwich

White Desert

'Great God! this in an awful place...'

  Scott, at the South Pole, 17 January 1912

Most people know the Moon better than Antarctica. The ice-bound continent at the far end of the world is the fifth largest, only Europe being smaller, but until the early 1800s it was as far beyond human imagination as it is beyond sight.

Antarctica's 5.5 million square miles (14.2 million sq. km) would cover the United States and Central America, while France and Britain together would fit easily into either of its two great bays, the Ross and Weddell Seas. Apart from small areas of the coastline and the peaks of its mountain ranges, it is permanently covered by some 7 million cubic miles of ice, lying on average between just under 1.25 and just over 2.25 miles thick. The ice sheet has been there for at least 25 million years. Its weight is so vast that, in places, it has pressed the underlying land mass hundreds of metres below sea level.

Over 90 per cent of the world's fresh water is locked up in the Antarctic ice. Were it to melt, the inhabitable planet would shrink unrecognizably as the oceans rose by between 150 and 200 ft, drowning most of the islands and coastal nations that we know. Of New York, London and other great maritime cities, only the abandoned shells of tall buildings would rise above the surface. Seen from these decaying grave markers, the view would often be of many new islands but with extensive land on distant horizons, if visible at all.

Antarctica would also look very different but still be the size of Australia and Indonesia. The peaks of the great Transantarctic Mountains would rise, as now, to between 6,500 to 13,000 ft over the rocky plateau of Eastern or Greater Antarctica. This is the older part of the continent, lying to the 'right' of the Greenwich and 180° meridians of longitude. Even below the ice this is still high ground, averaging about 1,500 ft above the sea. Western or Lesser Antarctica, the geologically younger area to the 'left' of longitudes 0/180°, which includes the 800-mile finger of the Antarctic Peninsula reaching towards South America, would by contrast have largely fragmented into an archipelago of islands between the enlarged Ross and Weddell Seas.

While the fossil record shows that prehistoric Antarctica was once a warm and life-rich zone, the prospect of a thaw making it one again is equally remote, man-made global warming aside. The ice and the rock beneath are inseparable and the continent is not only by far the coldest place on earth but also the highest, the mean height of its frozen surface

Opposite: Adélie penguin and sledging tracks converge on the Ross Ice Shelf. Photograph by Herbert Ponting, *Terra Nova* expedition.

Emperor penguins. Photograph by Frank Hurley, *Endurance* expedition.

above the sea being between 7,000 and 8,000 ft. This is over twice as high as Asia, its nearest rival at 3,000 ft on average. The South Pole itself is 9,500 ft high, so the European race to it was in no sense one between competitors and climate on a level playing field: it was a climb to, and endurance at, an altitude that is usually the province of mountaineers.

How the polar ice sheet originally formed is the subject of at least five theories. That it endures is partly due to its massive thermal inertia and altitude, and to the fact that such direct solar heat as it receives during the brief Antarctic summer is reflected by its own whiteness into space, rather than absorbed. Much also has to do with its being surrounded by the cold but biologically teeming waters of the Southern Ocean – the resource, in terms of whaling and sealing, that led to man's first commercial interest in the region in the nineteenth century.

Most remarkable, perhaps, is how little appears to sustain the mainland ice coverage. Antarctic cloud, drawn in from the warmer ocean to the north, is high and thin, another factor preventing heat retention. Rain is practically unknown save occasionally on the coast and snowfall is surprisingly light. On average, snow equivalent to only about 6.5 in. of water falls in a year. Perhaps less than 2 in. falls near the Pole, for inland the high-altitude cold makes the air about ten times drier than in temperate areas of the world. Very little melts however, since most of the continent stays well below freezing. It is a vast, dry and intensely cold desert, built up layer on minute layer over unimaginable time. Nothing decays: mummified seals several thousand years old have been found well inland. One of Scott's dogs still guards his base camp nearly a century after its death, teeth bared in a desiccated snarl. Dead men endure, freeze-dried, as does all normally biodegradable waste. The only indigenous plants are a scattering of highly adapted lichens and mosses clinging to exposed rock, mostly around the coast. All other life is sustained in or from the sea, with seal and penguin species the only large animals that breed on the mainland.

In the deep Antarctic winter months of August and September mean temperatures range from –20 to –30°C on the coast and from –40 to –70°C inland. In summer the interior remains between –20 and –35°C, with the coast hovering around freezing point, although the Antarctic Peninsula can see brief rises to 15°C (59°F). By contrast 0°C and –20 to –35°C are, respectively, the normal summer and winter mean temperatures of the much warmer Arctic, which is a frozen ocean surrounded by continental landmasses and Antarctica's complete physical, as much as polar opposite. The lowest temperatures on earth, –89.2°C (1983) on the high interior and –60°C near sea level, are Antarctic records. At such temperatures fuel oil congeals like jelly,

> if you drop a steel bar it is likely to shatter like glass, tin disintegrates into loose granules, mercury freezes into solid metal, and if you haul up a fish through a hole in the ice within five seconds it is frozen so solid that it has to be cut with a saw

John Bechervaise, *The Far South*, 1962

New leads covered with ice flowers in early spring with *Endurance* seen in the distance.

By far the worst aspect of the cold in human terms is the additional effect of 'wind-chill', for every knot of wind-speed is the physiological equivalent to a drop of one degree in temperature. Frostbite in such conditions is a routine danger and rapid hypothermic death a penalty for accidents or failures of planning. These are hazards that Scott and Shackleton's generation was neither the first nor the last to face with only natural types of clothing – none with the thermal efficiency of modern synthetics.

Wind is ever present in Antarctica. The surrounding Southern Ocean is the stormiest in the world, with a 15-ft swell normal in calm conditions. Perpetual gales and cyclonic storms generated around the 'Antarctic Convergence' of cold polar air and seas with warmer ones, at about latitude 50° south, chase each other endlessly west to east around the world, creating huge seas that sweep on, unimpeded by intervening land save the few sub-Antarctic islands. The 'roaring forties' latitudes, in which clippers like *Cutty Sark* drove eastward on the Australian wool-run and home round Cape Horn, merge with the 'frightful fifties', where the average windspeed is 37.7 knots – a Force 8 gale. From here south, not-withstanding the wind, endemic Convergence fogs and the increased risks of ice add to hazards with which only modern ships are fully equipped to cope.

In the high mainland interior winds are relatively light but from there heavy cold air pours down to the coast creating fierce local storms. At worst, these 'katabatic' (descending) winds can average over 100 miles an hour and have been measured in gusts of over 150. They easily become turbulent, and while no new snow is involved, they whip up the granular surface crystals formed by recent falls into lethal sub-zero blizzards. It was in such conditions on the low-lying Ross Ice Shelf that Scott's party died in 1912.

Not only wind pours off the highlands. So, too, in longer timescale does the ice itself, in the spectacular coastal glaciers that formed early explorers' gateways to the interior. Of these the 100-mile Beardmore and the nearby Axel Heiberg Glaciers are (though not the largest) forever linked as Scott's and Amundsen's routes up to the Pole. They and five others flow down at a rate of about 1,100ft a year to feed the Ross Ice Shelf, which fills the landward end of the Ross Sea. This – also called the Great Ice Barrier – is the largest of a dozen that make up about a third of the Antarctic coastline. At 310,000 sq. miles it is larger than France and ranges from 2,000ft thick on the landward side to 600ft at seaward. The Ronne Ice Shelf in the Weddell Sea – named after its American discoverer, Finn Ronne (1947) – is next largest at just under 12,750 square miles (this excludes the smaller Filchner Ice Shelf to the east of Berkner Is.). From the 'ice front' or outer edge of the shelves, which can present cliffs of over 100ft to approaching ships, table-top icebergs more than a mile long routinely calve off and float over 2,000 miles north before breaking up, which can take five years. They can be of even vaster size, 90 miles in one measured instance, and sometimes make spectacular appearances off the South African coast.

The main Barrier ice and bergs are of fresh water, being formed originally from compacted snow. The seasonal pack-ice, which is far more dynamic in its movement and covers the greatest area, forms by a complex process from seawater into sheets of up to about 6in. thick, rising to 6ft or more if it survives for over two years. By the time it has lasted three years it is 'old ice' and has lost its surface salinity, providing good drinking water. The mainland lies almost entirely within the Antarctic Circle (66°33' south – the outer limit of 24-hour polar daylight in summer and darkness in winter) but the winter pack – at maximum extent in August and September – reaches north to latitude 54° in the Atlantic, 56°-59° in the Indian Ocean sector and 60°-63° in the Pacific, the Antarctic Convergence in both the last two being further south. At 60 nautical (or 69 statute) miles to each degree and expanding in all directions northward, these are vast areas and can be greater in a severe season. Seen from space, the winter area of the Antarctic ice can practically double. However, there are astonishing variations, famously exemplified by the Scottish sealer James Weddell's

Photograph showing 'foot stalactites' recorded during the *Endurance* expedition.

penetration of the sea that bears his name in 1823, when he reached just over 74° south without encountering significant ice at all.

Linear distances are also daunting. The tip of the Antarctic Peninsula is 600 miles south of Cape Horn across the stormy Drake passage but,

Panorama of pinnacle or moraine ice, *Terra Nova* expedition.

isolated islands apart, New Zealand is the next closest land at 2,100 miles away. South Africa is some 2,500 miles, with the south coast of Australia around 2,300 miles away. Lesser and Greater Antarctica together, measured west-to-east through the Transantarctic range, are about 2,800 miles across at their widest. The narrow land neck connecting them between the Ross and Weddell seas is under 600, excluding the ice-shelves which make the sea-to-sea distance far wider.

The first crossing of the continent was the highly mechanized Commonwealth Trans-Antarctic Expedition of 1957–58 under Dr Vivian Fuchs and Sir Edmund Hillary, fulfilling Shackleton's dream of linking the Weddell and Ross Seas via the South Pole. Fuchs started on the Weddell ice-edge and covered the 2,180 miles to the Scott Base at McMurdo Sound in 99 days. Hillary's party, laying depots from McMurdo to the Pole and returning with Fuchs, was the first since Scott's to reach it overland. The US Amundsen-Scott Polar Base had just been built, in 1956–57, by air drop from McMurdo as part of the International Geophysical Year (IGY) programme. The (then) Geomagnetic South Pole and the separate Pole of Relative Inaccessibility – the furthest point from the sea that can be reached, 12,000 feet up and 1,250 miles inland (lat. 82° 06' south, long.

54° 58' east) – were both attained by a land-based Soviet team over two seasons in 1957–58, in their contribution to the IGY. Since then two further land expeditions have crossed the continent. The first, a three-man party led by Sir Ranulph Fiennes and using sledge-pulling 'ski-doos', took 67 days in 1980–81, broadly following the 0/180° meridians as part of their British Transglobe Expedition. An international six-man party using dog teams and led by the American, Will Steger, took seven months in 1989–90 to cover some 3,750 miles from the tip of the Peninsula, via the Pole, to the Russian Mirny Base on the eastern coast.

By comparison, Amundsen's high-speed dash from the Ross sea up the Axel Heiberg Glacier with dogs and skis, which won the race to the Pole was about 810 miles (700 nautical miles): Scott's tragic, trudging march to it up the Beardmore Glacier, the *via dolorosa* of Antarctic discovery as one writer has called it, was 880 miles (about 760 nautical miles).

Looking south

Terra Australis recenter inventa sed nondum plene cognita

This optimistic Latin description, meaning 'Southern Land recently discovered but not yet fully known', first appeared on an imagined map of Antarctica in 1531. Its basis was twofold: a belief inherited from Classical times that an icy southern zone must exist to 'balance' the cold northern regions and Magellan's passage in 1520 through the southern straits that now bear his name, during the first voyage round the world. This left the false impression that Tierra del Fuego was the tip of something much bigger. Somewhere in the preceding centuries the Classical notion of 'Terra Australis' being icy transformed into one of its being a more temperate 'counterweight' to northern lands and a potentially rich prize for its discoverers.

During the *Golden Hind*'s circumnavigation of 1577–80, Francis Drake was driven well south of Cape Horn in 1578 into what is now the Drake Passage and clearly reported wide open seas and 'no maine or iland to be seen to the southwards'. However, neither this nor later southern island discoveries finally dislodged the myth of a temperate polar continent until the 1770s.

In that era of European commercial, colonial and, finally, ideological warfare, scientific navigation came into its own as a tool by which new lands could be found, fixed, claimed and drawn into an imperial embrace. Britain and France were the new contenders, with Spain defending a long-standing oceanic empire. In 1768–70 Lieutenant James Cook's *Endeavour* voyage – a scientific one to observe the transit of Venus across the Sun from Tahiti – also charted New Zealand. This proved that it, too, was no part of a polar continent, as Tasman had done for Australia in the early 1640s. With a recent history of both Spanish and French activity in southern latitudes, the government then decided to send Cook to resolve the 'Southern Continent' issue for good and, if it existed, claim it for

Captain James Cook (1728-79), by Nathaniel Dance (1735-1811).

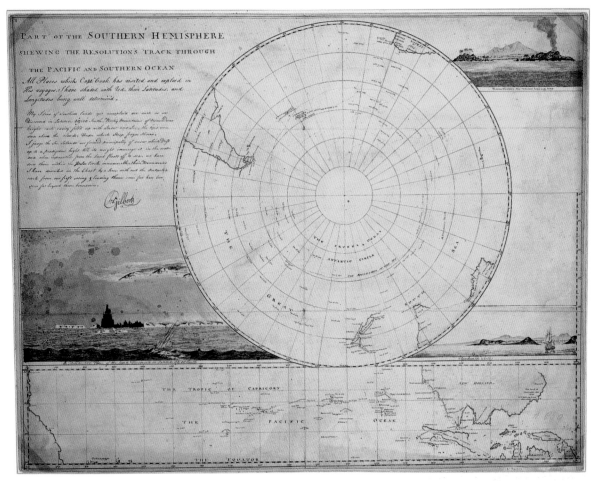

Britain. Armed this time with John Harrison's newly perfected chronometer, to fix accurate longitude at sea, Cook's ships *Resolution* and *Adventure* spent the two antipodean summers of 1772–74 pushing as far south as ice, fog and endurance would allow.

It was the first modern Antarctic expedition: Cook approached from the Atlantic and Pacific, circumnavigating the continent without seeing it, though coming almost within sight at his most southerly point, latitude 71° 10' in 1773–74 – one not reached again in that area until 1959–60. He returned with the first detailed account of pack-ice and 'ice islands' (icebergs) and a belief that a cold land-mass entirely within the 60th parallel south was their likely source. Based on his discovery of desolate South Georgia in 1775 he also said, with Yorkshire pragmatism, that such a continent might not be worth finding.

Cook died on Hawaii in 1779, with France already at war with Britain (until 1783) as an ally of the American rebels. The French Revolutionary War itself began in 1793 and it was not until after Napoleon's defeat in 1815 that the Royal Navy began to think again of polar exploration. It had established a Hydrographic Office in 1795 to make official charts and had a large number of under-employed younger officers seeking peacetime opportunities for glory. The period 1823–54, with Sir Francis Beaufort as Hydrographer (he of the Beaufort Scale for wind speeds), was a great period of Royal Naval surveying. It was also one of Arctic exploration as naval expeditions, the first in 1819, revived the sixteenth-century quest for a North-West Passage around North America, between the Atlantic and Pacific. From 1847 this effectively became a series of search parties (not all British or official) to discover the fate of Captain Sir John Franklin's expedition, which had left on the same quest in 1845 in Her Majesty's ships *Erebus* and *Terror*, and had vanished without trace. The total loss of Franklin's party of 129 was only confirmed in 1859, and although in the process the existence of an ice-bound North-West Passage was also established in 1850, it proved impassable to large sailing ships. Amundsen would be the first to sail through in the small *Gjøa* in 1903–06. The last major Royal Naval Arctic and scientific expedition tried to reach the North Pole in 1875–76 under Captain Sir George Nares, who had already seen Antarctic waters. Sledges reached 83° 20' north, but the Navy then rightly concluded there was no easy ice free sea passage to the Pole, and Arctic discovery was largely left to other nations and private interests.

There is some doubt about who first sighted the 'Antarctic continent', a phrase first speculatively used by Lieutenant Charles Wilkes, who was commodore of a seven-ship American naval expedition in 1838. The question, indeed, was still 'Is there a continent at all?'. The two contenders are Lieutenant Thaddeus von Bellingshausen of the Imperial Russian Navy, who went south in 1819–21 with two ships and orders to make discoveries as close as possible to the Pole, and the British naval lieutenant, Edward Bransfield. The honour, by three days, on 27 January 1820, appears to be Bellingshausen's but he never made such a claim, and his thorough work – which clarified what Cook had seen of the Antarctic islands, especially South Georgia and the South Sandwich group – sank little noticed after his return.

At the same time commercial sealers, tipped off by Cook's reports, were already beginning to decimate the fur seal population from South Georgia to the South Shetlands. The latter were discovered in 1819 by William Smith, Master of the British merchant vessel *Williams*, who was blown southwards off-course during a trading voyage from Buenos Aires to Valparaiso. Bransfield returned with him in January 1820, claiming them for Britain. On the 30th he sighted the tip of the Antarctic Peninsula, and he was certainly the first to chart part of the mainland. In 1822–24 the sealer James Weddell, as already mentioned, found unusually open water far into the 'Sea of George IV' as he called it – now the Weddell Sea – but sealing became uneconomic in the 1830s and it was the whalers who made the next contributions to knowledge.

The most notable of many was the firm of Samuel Enderby and Son –

Sir James Clark Ross (1800-62), by John R. Wildman (active 1823-39).

HMS *Erebus* and *Terror* in the Antarctic, 1847, by John Wilson Carmichael (1800-68).

based at Greenwich from 1834 – who had opened up the British South Pacific whale fishery as far back as 1775. They were a successful concern, promoting discovery well beyond commercial justification because of their own geographical interests. One of their captains, John Biscoe, circumnavigated Antarctica in 1831–32 with the ships *Tula* and *Lively*, sighting and naming Enderby Land and further defining the west coast of the Peninsula, which he called Graham Land. Other Enderby discoveries followed but by the time of Queen Victoria's accession in 1837 a combination of scientific interest and the whaling potential had revived official involvement.

Over the next six years there were three naval expeditions in Antarctica: French, British and American. The first two were under Captain Dumont d'Urville and Captain Sir James Clark Ross, who had reached the North Magnetic Pole in 1831, and were aimed unsuccessfully at finding its southern equivalent. (This was first done in 1909 by Edgeworth David, on Shackleton's *Nimrod* expedition, though the magnetic poles are migrating and rapidly alter position.) Dumont d'Urville found the mainland coast in longitudes 120–160^0 east, naming it Terre Adélie after his wife and, more indirectly, its inhabitants too – the Adélie penguins. Extraordinarily, he met but did not speak with the *Porpoise* of Wilkes's ill-equipped American Pacific expedition, which spent two difficult seasons investigating the southern whale fishery and also charted the coast now named after him.

Ross's hand-picked Royal Naval party of 1839–41 and 1842–43 was by contrast very well-found, sailing in the two specially strengthened ships, *Erebus* and *Terror*, which were later to vanish with Franklin. Their first two seasons were the most productive, especially from January 1841 when Ross discovered and claimed the coast of what is now the Ross Dependency, with the Ross Sea and 'Great Ice Barrier' (the Ross Ice Shelf). Here he named many of the features that were to become familiar in the saga of Scott and Amundsen. These included Possession Island, Cape Adare on the western side of the Ross Sea, the volcanoes Mounts Erebus and Terror on Ross Island (the former being active), and the sheltered McMurdo Sound that lies between there and the mainland. Ross's discoveries made his Antarctic expedition the most important of the century and there is a strange irony in his ships' disappearance so soon afterwards in the greatest-ever Arctic disaster.

Ross's success notwithstanding, the fragments of coast, ice and offshore islands so far discovered did not add up to proof of a single southern land mass. This remained the case until after the round-the-world oceanographic research voyage of HMS *Challenger*, under Sir George Nares, in 1874–75. *Challenger*'s brief foray into the Antarctic was a minor part of her programme but she was the first steam vessel to cross the Antarctic Circle and, while Nares did not see the mainland, deep-sea geological samples that he brought home proved to be of continental origin dropped out to sea by glacial movement. There was a continent there, its outline still unknown save for the few coastal points so far fixed on the chart.

During the next twenty years a few whalers went south into the region, searching for new grounds. The northern fishery was becoming exhausted but with steam and the Norwegian Svend Foyn's invention of the harpoon gun revolutionizing the industry, it once more looked southwards in earnest. On the east of the Antarctic Peninsula, the Larsen Ice Shelf commemorates the last great explorer whaling captain, the Norwegian Carl Larsen, who discovered much of the area and whose reports persuaded Foyn, in 1894, to back a further voyage by Henrik Bull in the whaler *Antarctic*. On 24 January 1895 Bull and his men were the first to make a confirmed landing on the continent proper, near Cape Adare. One of them was a young Norwegian seaman and childhood friend of Amundsen called Carsten Borchgrevink. In 1898 his so-called 'British Antarctic Expedition' was landed at Cape Adare from the whaler *Southern Cross*, to become the first to pass a winter on the mainland. Despite its name – required by its British sponsor, the publisher Sir George Newnes – Borchgrevink's party was largely Norwegian, one of whom died. When their ship collected them in January 1900, they briefly went further south. Here Borchgrevink, the English merchant naval officer William Colbeck, and a Finn, sledged 10 miles over the Ross Sea Barrier to 78° 50' south, the nearest to the Pole yet reached by man. The first ship to winter in the

The *Belgica* trapped in the ice of the Bellingshausen Sea, midwinter 1898.

Antarctic – the *Belgica* under the Belgian Lieutenant Adrien de Gerlache – had then already wintered too, but by accident. In 1898–99 she was trapped for a year in the pack-ice of the Bellingshausen Sea, west of the Antarctic Peninsula. It was a terrible experience for all concerned, including the Norwegian second mate Roald Amundsen.

At the same time money was being raised in London to launch what would be Scott's first expedition of 1901, in the *Discovery*. The moving spirit was Sir Clements Markham, President of the Royal Geographical Society since 1893 but, as a former naval midshipman, a veteran of both the Franklin search (under Captain Horatio Austin in 1850–51) and of the British Antarctic Expedition of 1875–76 commanded by Sir George Nares, which he had accompanied as far as Greenland. He had come a long way since the Franklin search, having left the Navy and despite some difficulties forged a successful career in what became the India Office. Here he was instrumental in starting quinine production in India, having organized the transplanting of chinchona trees from Peru, and was lent as geographer to a British punitive expedition in Ethiopia. A domineering and determined personality but also a brilliant communicator, to whom the deeds of great

William Colbeck's sledging flag from Borchgrevink's Antarctic expedition of 1898. (71cm x 91.5cm, 28ins x 36ins)

explorers were meat and drink, Markham was Secretary of the Royal Geographical Society before becoming President and making a British Antarctic expedition the aim of his Presidency. The purpose was to widen geographical and scientific knowledge of the continent but, based on his

Pancake ice and 'mini-bergs' photographed by Frank Debenham, *Terra Nova* expedition.

own experience and that of the *Challenger*, he took it as axiomatic that the Admiralty was the best organization to undertake and finance the task, and that a naval officer should be the leader. He did not plan a race for the Pole but was also clear that Britain must get there first if contention arose.

Markham presided over the Sixth International Geographical Conference in London in 1895 which placed priority on Antarctic discovery as 'the greatest piece of geographical exploration still to be undertaken'. It rankled when Borchgrevink, fresh from Bull's expedition, arrived to address the conference rather less than modestly about their first landing at Cape Adare in January and his own plans for what became the *Southern Cross* voyage. This Markham tried to impede but was frustrated by Newnes's sponsorship of it – all the more galling when his initial approaches for government support for his own plans were rebuffed.

From his Presidential chair Markham none the less persuaded the Royal Geographical Society to put up £5,000 as seed-corn for a public appeal and the Royal Society to lend its support, early in 1898. The following year a wealthy industrial sponsor called Llewellyn Longstaff, also a keen geographer and Fellow of the RGS, came forward to add £25,000 to the £14,000 by then collected. Finance was assured when the Treasury promised £45,000 in 'match-funding' to a similar private sum, which was already practically obtained. In all, £93,000 was raised.

What Markham now needed was a leader in his required mould. Walking home down the Buckingham Palace Road in June 1899, a chance encounter with someone he had first met over ten years earlier resolved his problem.

Discovery and Nimrod

[The Commander] must be a *naval officer*... and he must be *young*. These are essentials. Such a commander should be a good *sailor* with some experience of ships under sail, a *navigator* with a knowledge of *surveying*, and he should be of *a scientific turn of mind*. He must have *imagination* and be capable of *enthusiasm*. His temperament must be *cool*, he must be *calm, yet quick and decisive* in action, *a man of resource, tactful* and *sympathetic*.

Sir Clements Markham

The man who crossed the road to greet Markham in 1899 was the torpedo lieutenant of the battleship *Majestic*, flagship of the Channel Squadron. It was within days of his thirty-first birthday and his name was Robert Falcon Scott.

Known to his family as 'Con', Scott was born at Stoke Damerel, Devonport, on 6 June 1868, the third of six children and the elder of two sons. His parents both had naval connections, although his father John owned a Plymouth brewery. 'Con' was a rather dreamy, self-sufficient boy, largely educated at home until he went, relatively late, to board at a Hampshire preparatory school known for taking those intended for the Navy. He joined the training ship *Britannia* in 1881 and, despite minor scrapes, was made cadet captain early in 1883 before passing out seventh in a class of twenty-six that summer, with first-class certificates in mathematics and seamanship. He was still a midshipman in November 1886 when he joined the training ship *Rover*, which took him out to the West Indies. It was here that he first came to the notice of Markham by winning a cutter race and being invited to dine with him in the squadron flagship, where Markham was a guest of his cousin, Admiral A.H. Markham, who had been second-in-command of Nares's Arctic expedition. Markam was impressed by his 'intelligence, information and the charm of his manner' – though Scott was not the only, or even the most favoured, 'mid' to fall under his calculating eye.

Confirmed as sub-lieutenant in 1888, Scott was posted to the cruiser *Amphion* in which he served in the Pacific and the Mediterranean, rising to lieutenant in 1889. Though he performed well, his letters at this time show he became depressed and dissatisfied both with the ship and himself, and probably realized that any prospect of a command was a long way off. He thus changed course into the new and more specialized path of torpedo warfare, training at Portsmouth before returning to the Mediterranean late in 1893 as torpedo lieutenant of the *Vulcan*, an experimental vessel. In the following autumn came the first of several family disasters.

John Scott had some years before sold his brewery to retire in gentlemanly comfort but the money had gone, through poor investment. The

Sir Clements Markham with Scott and his wife Kathleen on the deck of the *Terra Nova*, 1910.

large family home had to be let: Scott's younger brother, Archie, gave up his commission in the Royal Artillery, and joined a local regiment in Nigeria where the pay was better and costs less. The sisters all found work: the eldest, Ettie, to her mother's disquiet, became an actress but soon married a Member of Parliament. Their sixty-three-year-old father resumed work as a Somerset brewery manager.

To be closer to home, Scott transferred to Portsmouth and in 1896 was serving in the *Empress of India* in the Channel Squadron when he again met Markham, this time a guest in the *Royal Sovereign* at Vigo when they were *en route* to Gibraltar. Now Sir Clements, he was renewing his campaign to mount a British Antarctic expedition following the initial Admiralty refusal to assist. Of this Scott heard a little more, though their ways quickly parted and the following year he transferred to the battleship *Majestic*.

Four months later, in July 1897, Scott's father died leaving just over £1,500 and the cost of supporting their mother fell largely on the two brothers. This tragedy and Scott's financial difficulties were compounded in 1898, when Archie also died of typhoid while on home leave. Scott now felt that he was burdened by ill fortune and that he had to find some way to advance himself more rapidly. It was in these circumstances that he met Markham in the street, heard that the National Antarctic Expedition seemed a real possibility and two days later formally applied to command it. His success brought him promotion to Commander – and in due course a further allowance.

Lieutenant Robert Falcon Scott, an early portrait.

It was nearly a year until Scott's appointment was confirmed by the Joint Committee of the Royal and Royal Geographical Societies, of which Markham was Vice-President. During this time Scott returned to *Majestic* under Captain Egerton, whose warm reference none the less pointed out that he had no knowledge of Polar work. The same period also marked the successful end to a number of long-running battles for Markham, including getting his way that the prime aim of the voyage would be geographical rather than oceanographic and that the commander of the ship would also command the expedition, not a scientist. This was difficult, since a distinguished geologist had already been invited to become Scientific Director but withdrew rather than take a subordinate role. Prime Minister Balfour's interest having finally secured Markham the official funding he sought, the Admiralty also agreed to provide another regular officer as second-in-command and two or three others from the Royal Naval Reserve. In fact they supplied rather more, let alone the bulk of the crew, most of whom were volunteers whom Scott had canvassed through friends in the Channel Squadron.

Notably he chose a number of men from the *Majestic*: Lieutenants Michael Barne and Reginald Skelton (as chief engineer), Warrant Officer James Dellbridge as second engineer, and two petty officers, David Allen and Edgar Evans, who was to be the first to die returning from the Pole in

Scott and the ship's company on the deck of *Discovery*, East India Dock, London, 16 September 1904, taken by 'Thomson'.

1912. The navigator and second-in-command was in the end a lieutenant RNR, a P&O officer called Albert Armitage who had been part of the Jackson-Harmsworth Arctic Expedition to Franz Josef Land (1894–97), while the first lieutenant, twenty-three-year-old Charles Royds, had recently been commanding a torpedo-boat destroyer. The last officer was a Merchant Navy second mate called Ernest Shackleton, making his Polar debut as a specially rated sub-lieutenant RNR. He came on leave from the Union Castle Line, having first used his considerable charm on the son of the expedition's main private sponsor, Longstaff, and then on Scott himself to secure a place. He had excellent experience in sail and steam, an outgoing personality and a natural leader's ability to get men working together. In the long term, however, these qualities would give rise to underlying tensions with Scott's reserve and tendency to irritability under stress.

The regular officers all had scientific functions – Royds being the meteorologist for example – but there was also a civilian scientific complement. Louis Bernacchi, a Tasmanian who had wintered at Cape Adare with Borchgrevink was the physicist, particularly concerned with the magnetic work, and joined the ship in New Zealand. Hartley Ferrar, a recent Cambridge graduate, and Thomas Vere Hodgson of the Plymouth Marine

Many fund-raising and celebratory dinners were held for *Discovery*. Photograph of the Mayor of Portsmouth's banquet held to celebrate the return of *Discovery* in Portsmouth, 13 September 1904.

Biological Laboratory came respectively as geologist and biologist. Dr Reginald Koettlitz (known as 'Cutlets' and at forty the oldest member of the expedition) had been with Armitage in the Arctic and was senior surgeon and botanist. His assistant, both medically and as naturalist was Dr Edward Adrian Wilson, the artistically gifted and deeply Christian peacemaker of both Scott's voyages, known ten years later as 'Uncle Bill'. Though initially closer to Shackleton, he was to become the confidant and companion on whom Scott, not himself religious and prone to self-doubts, came most personally to rely: 'a brave, true man – the best of comrades and the staunchest of friends' as he wrote to Wilson's wife when both lay dying in their tent in 1912.

The question of what vessel would be used was faced by the Ship Committee long before Scott appeared. The committee was chaired by Admiral Sir Leopold McClintock who, as a lieutenant, had solved the Franklin riddle forty years before. Markham had known him since those days and was much influenced by him (and was later his biographer). McClintock's method of man-hauling sledges – which employed the manpower available to him – had subsequently become a practical orthodoxy for Royal Naval Arctic expeditions and, less justifiably, one

The launch of the *Discovery* at Dundee, 21 March 1901.

which time hallowed with 'manly' moral weight. In hindsight, this is difficult fully to understand given that McClintock was a good dog driver and that Naval expeditions back to Parry's in the early 1820s had experience of dogs from Inuit practice, some copying it. Part of the answer lies in numerical ratios: dogs are most effective as 'primary traction' when few men are involved. Otherwise the number of dogs required becomes impractical. In the matter of a ship, however, the experience of McLintock and his colleagues produced a winner.

Markham himself visited Norway in 1898, as did Scott, to consult the explorer Fridtjof Nansen about potential steamships and to look at the possibility of having a vessel built similar to the *Fram*, in which Nansen had made his own epic voyage towards the North Pole in 1893–96. Later Amundsen's ship, she was designed to be squeezed up out of heavy pack-ice that might threaten to crush her. This came to nothing, as did the idea of using various wooden whalers, including the old *Bloodhound*, which as HMS *Discovery* had been one of the ships taken to the Arctic in 1875–76 by another Ship Committee member, Sir George Nares. The end result was that a new wooden steam-auxiliary sailing ship was designed based on Nares's *Discovery*, though with significant modifications. Principal among them was a massively strengthened 'ice–breaker' bow, a rounded over-hanging stern to resist ice pressure and a carefully calculated use of ferrous metals to make the vessel a suitable platform to conduct geomagnetic experiments. Designed by Sir William Smith and laid down by the Dundee

Officers (left) and crew (right) pose for pictures at the stern of *Discovery*, in Lyttelton harbour, New Zealand.

Shipbuilders Company, well experienced in building Polar whalers, the new auxiliary barque was both one of the last three-masted wooden ships to be built and the first specially for scientific use since the little *Paramore* in 1694, constructed for a voyage under the astronomer Edmond Halley. She was 172 ft long, 33 ft in the beam and of 1,570 tons, with sides 26 in. thick and a coal-fired 450 i.h.p.(indicated horsepower) triple-expansion engine. On 21 March 1901, with Markham, Scott and many others present, Lady Markham launched her at Dundee as the *Discovery* – a name first borne to the Antarctic by one of Cook's ships in the 1770s.

Moonlight view of *Discovery* in winter at Hut Point.

Discovery sailed from London on 31 July 1901, cheered by large crowds and provisioned to support forty-seven men for three years – much of her supplies being donated by commercial sponsors. Off Cowes, King Edward VII came aboard with Queen Alexandra and invested Scott with the Royal Victorian Order. On 3 October she stopped briefly to refit and replenish stores at Cape Town *en route* for Lyttelton, New Zealand, where she docked on 29 November. On the way, to begin the magnetic survey work, Scott diverted far south over the 60th parallel, encountered their first ice and called at deserted Macquarie Island, where the crew reacted well to the addition of penguin to their diet. The ship proved a slow sailer and heavy on coal when steaming but was otherwise an excellent sea-boat in the worst conditions. At Lyttelton her rigging was reset and stores replenished, with the gift of forty-five live sheep being added to the twenty-three sledge dogs carried on deck. Again cheered by crowds, she sailed on 21 December, though immediately put into Port Chalmers to bury a seaman called Charles Bonner who was killed falling from the masthead. He and a

deserter were replaced by two volunteers from an accompanying warship, HMS *Ringarooma*. One was AB Thomas Crean, henceforth the most indestructible and permanent figure in both Scott and Shackleton's stories. With Stoker William Lashly, whom he now first met, he was to be

'General Flat Race on Skis. Distance: 2 miles, 4 prizes'.

one of the heroes of Scott's last expedition.

On 2 January 1902 *Discovery* saw her first icebergs and began to push through a 270-mile belt of pack-ice, amid which the crew tried their skis and slaughtered the sheep, seals and penguin for the larder, now that the cold would preserve the results. Scott's squeamishness about such necessary butchery is well recorded: compared to Amundsen who routinely killed sledge dogs to feed the other dogs – and his men – it was a significant weakness. On 8 January they landed near Cape Adare, visiting Borchgrevink's hut, before sailing on to seek winter quarters further south. They found McMurdo Sound full of ice, and on 23 January, after establishing a mail-drop for their relief ship *Morning* at Cape Crozier on Ross Island (which they later first recognized as such), they sailed east along the edge of the Ice Barrier itself. This had now receded since Ross first found it but was generally from 50 to 240 feet high above the sea. On the 26th *Discovery* reached her furthest point south, latitude 78 ° 36', and on the 30th Scott realized both from soundings and crags visible up to 2,000 feet that they had discovered the eastern coast of the Ross Sea, naming it King Edward VII Land. Turning back on 1 February, they briefly stopped in a 3-mile inlet in the ice-front and from here a sledging party reached latitude 79 ° 03'.5 to examine the surface. Here, too, Scott and Shackleton created another first, going up by balloon to survey the limitless plain. They saw no land in any direction, and Scott, who ascended first, nearly vanished for good by dropping too much ballast. Fortunately, the balloon was securely tethered but it developed a leak and was never used again.

Discovery returned to McMurdo Sound, which had cleared sufficiently
to anchor her in a sheltered inlet at what became known as Hut Point, near
the south end of Ross Island. By the end of March the ship was safely

'Xmas Celebrations on board *Discovery*',
December 1901.

The *Discovery*'s balloon, *Eva*, being inflated at
Barrier Inlet, February 1902.

frozen in with huts erected ashore for auxiliary accommodation (though
everyone in fact lived in the ship) and as observatories. By then George
Vince, a seaman, had been killed while on an abortive mission led by
Royds to leave messages for *Morning* at Cape Crozier. He, Evans and others
had been sent back in deteriorating weather when they slipped on a steep
slope. Vince disappeared into the icy sea. Clarence Hare, the steward, was
also presumed dead until he walked in over 36 hours later, having survived
that time in the open. Experience was proving the best of teachers but the
costs were heavy. Before the winter night finally descended, everyone
began to learn to ski and tried to get the dogs to work as sledge teams. In
both cases the British were novices, to a degree now almost unimaginable,
in skills that were almost native (certainly the skiing) to their Scandinavian
compeers. Scott found skiing 'a most pleasurable and delightful exercise'
but was not convinced at first that it would be useful when dragging
sledges; and despite liking his dogs he was not at ease with their savagery
and the ruthlessness needed to manage them. For both Scott and
Shackleton the cultural prejudice in favour of man-hauling sledges or using
hardy ponies rather than dogs, against the urging of their Norwegian
colleagues, was to prove near-fatal in their first voyages and, with other
factors, finally so for Scott in 1911–12.

Aside from regular scientific observations and the normal business of
living, winter was taken up with activities that had been Naval traditions in
the Arctic: amateur theatricals in the 'Royal Terror Theatre' (the hut) were

Scott, Shackleton and Wilson before departure on the southern journey in November 1902.

one high point while Shackleton, as editor, and Wilson, as illustrator, put out five eagerly awaited typed editions of the *South Polar Times*. Too little time was spent on practical preparation for the spring but Scott did a great deal of relevant reading and laid plans for travelling south when light returned.

Scott's first sortie with two companions was a disaster. Two days later they struggled back with frostbite after their tent blew away in temperatures of –50°C. The next try saw him, Shackleton and Thomas Feather lay a large depot 85 miles south of the ship. Feather fell down a crevasse, from which Scott rescued him with difficulty. On their return they found that scurvy had made its appearance among another party that had explored to the westward, living primarily on pemmican, a high energy mixture of dried beef and lard that was a staple of all British polar expeditions. Scurvy was not then understood as a dietary deficiency, though fresh meat was known to prevent it, which led to a further round of seal hunting. On 2 November 1901, Scott, Shackleton and Wilson – with nineteen dogs, skis and five sledges – struck out on a major journey southwards, the Pole being the unstated objective. A second party of twelve under Barne man-hauled in parallel with them to lay further depots until 15 November.

It was to prove a painful journey. The energy of the dogs soon waned: they had begun undernourished from having too little fresh meat in their winter feed, while the stockfish being carried for them on Nansen's advice was both inadequate and partly contaminated due to poor storage *en route*. They soon began to die, forcing Wilson to feed the dead to the living and begin killing the weaker ones for the same purpose. Wilson rapidly became agonizingly snow blind from unwise sketching and Shackleton developed an ominous cough, eventually spitting blood. Scott and Shackleton's personalities – the one taciturn, the other volatile – began to

'Return of the Captain from the southern journey', February 1903, greeted by Reginald Koettlitz.

grate on each other as they crossed the featureless Barrier, Wilson finding himself the moderating influence. Scott had miscalculated the amount of pemmican they needed and both hunger and scurvy began to bite. On 30 December, after celebrating Christmas with a miniature plum pudding brought by Shackleton, they had to turn back at 82° 17' south, still 410 miles from the Pole. Having killed the last dogs they were by then hauling their remaining sledges until, about 150 miles from home, Shackleton became incapable of doing more than stagger along on his own, occasionally sitting on the last sledge to act as a brake. In this desperate state, on 3 February, they met Skelton and Bernacchi who had come south to find them. In all they had travelled about 850 miles, had been away for ninety-three days and had completed the longest sledging journey yet in Antarctica, as well as far exceeding the record for furthest south. They were all suffering from scurvy, exhaustion and malnutrition and Shackleton's rapid decline had raised serious questions about his basic constitution and fitness.

On return to base they found that the *Morning* had arrived with orders for *Discovery* to sail for Lyttelton. But she could not be broken from the ice and, rather than persist, Scott decided to spend another southern winter at Hut Point. When *Morning* sailed on 2 March she took eight men with her and Shackleton, whom Scott ordered home on medical grounds, though the tensions which had begun to emerge on their southern journey were also probably a contributing factor.

During Scott's absence Armitage had discovered a way up through the coastal mountains to the ice sheet of Victoria Land and the following October, 1903, Scott led a party up on to it. Again blizzards reduced temperatures to −50°C and broken sledges caused a false start. When they set out again they then lost a vital navigational handbook in bad weather and took a great risk in continuing, eventually up to a height of 8,900 feet. In mid-December, with the party now divided into two, Scott, Lashly and Evans refound the Ferrar Glacier (which they had ascended to reach the plateau) by the expedient of falling 300 feet down one of its upper slopes. Fortunately no-one was hurt and Scott and Evans had an even more miraculous escape when they fell into a deep crevasse lower down, from which Lashly helped both escape. They returned to *Discovery* on 24 December after 81 days and 1,098 miles of successful sledging – significantly, without dogs – to find that various other parties had also done well in other directions; Wilson to Cape Crozier investigating Emperor penguins, Royds and Bernacchi east over the Barrier, Armitage surveying the Koettlitz Glacier. Lieutenant George Mulock, who had replaced Shackleton from the *Morning*, had surveyed over 200 mountains, consolidating the picture of the 300 miles of coastline that the expedition as a whole added to the map.

Scott's worry was now whether *Discovery* would be freed from the ice to sail with *Morning*, when she again arrived from Lyttelton. There were 20 miles of it between her and open water at the beginning of January 1904 when he and Wilson made a sortie northwards to investigate. What they found on the 5th was not only the *Morning* but also another ship, the larger *Terra Nova*, accompanying her, both sent by the Admiralty following much debate and anxiety at home about the expedition's safety. Scott now received firm orders that if the ice persisted *Discovery* was to be abandoned. It proved to be touch-and-go, with the ship still beset by about two miles of it in early February. Then on the 14th, the combined effects of ocean swell and explosives allowed the relief vessels to reach her. Two days later *Discovery* was completely free, the last alarm being when a gale drove her pounding onto a shoal as they were manoeuvring out round Hut Point on the 17th. For Scott 'the hours that followed were truly the most dreadful I have ever spent', but the situation was saved by a shift of current and with only relatively minor damage. All three ships headed north for New Zealand, *Morning* under sail since Captain Colbeck (Borchgrevink's companion) had given up much of her coal to *Discovery*. They entered Lyttelton together to a rapturous welcome on Good Friday, 1 April 1904.

The expedition had made the first long-distance penetration of the Antarctic continent and the scientific results – geographical, geological, biological and in areas such as magnetic surveying and meteorology – were substantial. They filled many volumes of publication and the existence

Discovery with Mount Erebus beyond.

today of the Scott Polar Research Institute at Cambridge is, in part, a longer term legacy of the work done under him on the *Discovery* voyage.

'The only comment he made to me about not reaching the Pole, was "a live donkey is better than a dead lion, isn't it?"...'

Emily Shackleton, 1922

Nimrod
1907–09

On Shackleton's return to England in June 1903 he was quickly drawn into the row caused by Scott's decision, contrary to instructions, to spend two winters in Antarctica: the failure to free *Discovery* from the ice was read as incompetence. This became a public one when, with expedition funds exhausted, the Admiralty felt obliged to underwrite a relief voyage, not only for *Morning* but to buy and send the *Terra Nova* as well. Under Markham's guidance Shackleton publicly defended the expedition and helped fit out *Terra Nova* but he declined to sail with her.

Shackleton had been born in Co. Kildare, Ireland, on 15 February 1874, to a landed but not wealthy Anglo-Irish, Protestant family. From 1880 they lived in Dublin and in 1884 his father, by then a doctor, moved them to Sydenham, south London. Ernest was the second child and, like Scott, the elder of two brothers, though with eight rather than four sisters. Like Scott, too, he was educated at home until he was eleven and then went on to Dulwich College – the local middle-class public school. He was not academic (though he loved reading and poetry, especially Browning) but was well liked, addicted to tales of adventurous romance, often in mild trouble and famously inventive in talking himself out of it. By sixteen he had decided he wanted to go to sea and – to cure this – his father's cousin

Members of the *Nimrod* expedition, reading copies of the *Illustrated London News*.

found him a berth as ship's boy in a square-rigger, outward bound round the Horn for Valparaiso. It confirmed rather than cured his seafaring streak: he signed on, spent the next four years in the same ship and qualified as a second mate. He then transferred to steam tramping, mainly to the Far East, and in April 1898 obtained a Master's Certificate, aged twenty-four. The following year he joined the Union Castle Line on the South Africa run, also becoming a Fellow of the Royal Geographical Society as a matter of personal interest in exploration.

Shackleton was third mate in the *Tintagel Castle* when, in 1900, he met Cedric Longstaff, son of the *Discovery* expedition's main private sponsor, going out with his regiment to the Boer War. By this time he had also fallen in love with Emily Dorman, a friend of one of his sisters, whose prosperous solicitor father liked him but thought his daughter could do better. A combination of restlessness, the appeal of patriotic adventure, and the wish to distinguish himself led him to volunteer for Scott's expedition, obtaining an introduction from young Longstaff to his father – also a Fellow of the RGS.

Scott's decision to order Shackleton home in 1902 was an affront both to his aspirations as an explorer and his professional self-esteem. It called his fitness into question and implied he had not been frank about it when joining the expedition. This was a sensitive point, for Shackleton avoided medical examinations if possible. Though physically and mentally tough, he seems to have had, or developed, an instinct that his constitution was suspect but refused to acknowledge it or seek the reasons. After the southern journey Koettlitz had formally examined him for Scott and inconclusively suggested asthmatic tendencies. Only his death, aged forty-seven, in 1922, was to show that he had long-standing coronary heart disease. When this began is unknown but neither his lifelong cigarette smoking nor the privations he willingly endured would have helped either condition.

He had also now seen Scott's quality as a leader. From his viewpoint, it was that of a reserved but ambitious naval officer, whose social charm masked devious traits, and whose authority was based on his position rather than exceptional leadership ability. The expedition had also had its fair share of problems, albeit the result of general inexperience. By contrast Shackleton had an easy, charismatic rapport with most of the party – both officers and men, as in his other ships – and a higher confidence in his own leadership abilities. He had no doubt that Scott's uneasiness with him underlay his banishment and this was confirmed when Scott returned home. In a major lecture and the published account of the *Discovery* expedition he implied that Shackleton's health underlay their failure to get further south in 1902, minimized his own and Wilson's debility and overstated how they had had to pull him to safety as a passenger on the sledge.

This was humiliation to Shackleton. He had not of course dwelt on his problems and had a position – in fact several – to maintain. In the interim he had become Secretary of the Royal Scottish Geographical Society, was briefly a parliamentary candidate, a journalist and involved in various other uncertain business ventures in which his self-presentation was his main asset. He had also at last married Emily, to win whom he had, in part, originally joined *Discovery*.

Almost as soon as he returned Shackleton unsuccessfully urged Markham to help him mount his own expedition to reach either Pole as a deliberate aim rather than under scientific cover. This would be his answer to Scott. Both of them remained civil in public but were henceforth to avoid each other. However, Scott's treachery (as Shackleton saw it) was not his sole spur: others included the dramatic Argentine rescue of Carl Larsen and Otto Nordenskjöld from the Weddell Sea in 1903, after their ship, *Antarctic*, was crushed by ice; also the return of the Scottish explorer, William Bruce, to the Clyde (and a welcome that Shackleton organized) from a successful private expedition in the same area; and Amundsen's first traverse of the North-West Passage in 1903–06. In the background, too, were ongoing American plans to reach the North Pole.

By February 1907 Shackleton had his wish, launching an entirely private Antarctic expedition on a sea of large commercial hopes and rather less ready money. A loan of £1,000 from an eccentric lady admirer, a £7,000 guarantee from the Scottish industrialist William Beardmore – for

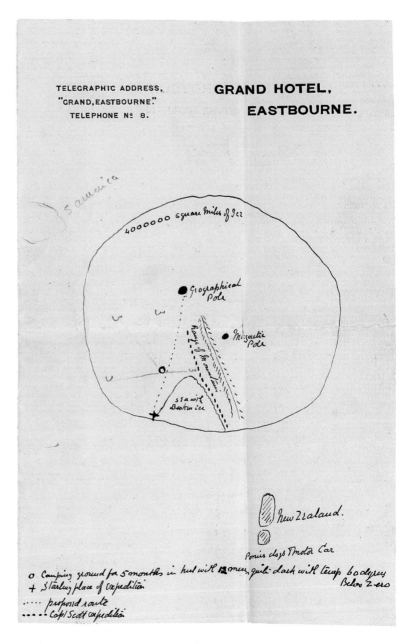

A sketch by Ernest Shackleton outlining his planned route to the Pole, probably done at a fund-raising dinner in 1907.

whom Shackleton briefly worked and whose wife was a close *confidante* – and the promise of backing from a mining speculator, who would obtain mineral rights to any such resources found, were the three main elements. Further returns were to come from the articles, lecturing, books and even film that Shackleton saw himself producing on his return.

The 'British Antarctic Expedition 1907' was organized with great speed, not least because Shackleton unsuccessfully urged both Wilson and Mulock to join him and found out from the latter that Scott was already thinking of a second southern venture. Shackleton realized that he would stand to lose from public confrontation with Scott and he sought to avoid it. One of his greatest disappointments was to find Wilson's moral weight firmly behind Scott's demand that he abandon his plan to use the McMurdo Sound base, to which Scott claimed exclusive rights. His greatest mistake, when Scott grandly extended his moral claims to the entire Victoria Land side of the Ross Sea, was to sign a written promise to base himself on the eastern side and under no circumstance stray west of the 170° meridian.

Shackleton's preparations were similar to Scott's yet also unlike. Rather than just scientists and regular naval men he recruited adventurers, some like himself of respectable background but most restless and unconventional. He visited Norway to obtain equipment and consulted Nansen, by then Norwegian minister in London, but ignored his and other Norwegian advice to use skis and dogs. The only dogs he took were nine picked up at the last minute in New Zealand. Instead he was persuaded by Frederick Jackson, and previous conversations with Armitage in *Discovery*, to buy twelve Manchurian ponies, despite the fact that Jackson's use of horses in Franz Josef Land had not been successful. This and the intention to walk not ski were more astonishing because his original idea was to march beyond the Pole, dragging a light boat, with which he planned to rejoin his ship at a rendezvous in the Weddell Sea. The boat was accidentally left behind but even Shackleton had realized that crossing the continent was too much to attempt. Beardmore, however, did fund a specially adapted car, the first to be used there: it did not match hopes, working to a useful degree on firm ground but immobilized by soft snow.

Shackleton remained bedevilled by inadequate finance, not least when his minerals backer failed to deliver. A final bizarre threat to his public credit arose when his shady businessman brother, Frank, was implicated in a high-profile scandal surrounding theft of the Irish coronation regalia early in 1907. As for a ship, all he could afford was a forty-year-old, 300-ton auxiliary sealer called *Nimrod,* which sailed from London on 30 July that year under the command of Rupert England, previously first mate of *Morning*.

Scott's well-funded expedition had been two years in the making: Shackleton's hand-to-mouth one took barely seven months. By royal command *Nimrod,* too, stopped in the Solent during Cowes week, under the guns of the Home Fleet drawn up in massive review. Edward VII and Queen Alexandra came aboard and Shackleton, like Scott, was made a Member of the Royal Victorian Order and presented with a Union flag by the Queen. *Nimrod* then sailed for New Zealand. Shackleton followed by steamer from Marseilles via Suez to Australia, after a last desperate round of fund-raising and a guilty farewell to the understanding Emily, left to manage with two small children on her own modest private means.

In Australia Shackleton made an immediate public hit, gaining much-needed support and recruiting the eminent, Welsh-born geologist Professor T.W. Edgeworth David, whose involvement secured him a £5,000 grant from the Australian government. With him came an old pupil, Douglas Mawson, whom Shackleton nominated as expedition physicist. Both had only originally asked to sail out and back in *Nimrod*, David's intention to

Bernard Day in the Arrol-Johnston car, supplied by William Beardmore for the *Nimrod* expedition.

remain with the landing party being undeclared until beyond reach. Both, too, were to gain Antarctic fame and knighthoods, Mawson at the head of later expeditions. New Zealand in turn supplied £1,000 and half the cost of towing *Nimrod* to the Antarctic when it was clear she was already too overloaded to carry enough coal and had to leave five ponies and other stores behind. The tow, by the *Koonya* under Frederick Evans, was an epic of skill, storm and appalling discomfort, ending on 15 January 1908 just inside the Antarctic Circle.

Shackleton's undertaking to base himself on the eastern side of the Ross Sea was immediately broken, to his own regret and with later public accusations of bad faith from Scott and his supporters. The Barrier edge had totally changed since 1902: *Discovery* or Barrier Inlet, where they had made the balloon ascent, had become part of a great bight which Shackleton named the Bay of Whales, while pack-ice and lack of coal prevented an extended search for a *terra firma* landing anywhere other than McMurdo Sound. Shackleton set up a base at Cape Royds, Ross Island, *Nimrod* being unable to reach Scott's anchorage at Hut Point because of ice. He and England seriously disagreed over the latter's handling of *Nimrod* in the difficult landing conditions, and on his return to Lyttelton England found that the sealed orders he was carrying from Shackleton dismissed him. When this news and that of the broken promise to Scott reached home, they combined with embarrassing revelations about both Frank Shackleton's affairs and Ernest's irregular use of expedition loans. Shackleton was now more than geographically isolated: debts were mounting, sponsors alienated and for a while even money for his relief by *Nimrod* was lacking.

Before winter set in, the only achievement at Cape Royds was a hazardously impromptu first ascent of Mount Erebus in March 1908. Eric Marshall, the surgeon, forbade Shackleton to undertake it unless passed fit. Shackleton declined to be examined and the climb was made by the fifty-four-year-old David, Mawson, Lieutenant Adams (the expedition second-in-command), both the doctors, Marshall and Mackay, and Sir Philip Brocklehurst, the twenty-year-old baronet adventurer of the party. This triumph of amateur mountaineering to the smoking crater, conducted without even proper boots and dogged by altitude sickness, fixed Erebus's height at 13,500ft.

Shackleton's style was very different from Scott's. There was no 'wardroom' and 'mess-deck' in his hut: everyone lived together, Shackleton's one distinction as leader being to have a personal sleeping cubicle. Amundsen was equally democratic. There were tensions, but his outward confidence and the courteous maturity of Edgeworth David maintained a working equilibrium through the winter, helped by Marshall's quite advanced dietary regime, which included both plenty of fresh seal meat and tinned fruit and tomatoes (all anti-scorbutic in effect). No serious attempt was made during these months to perfect the use of skis or the dogs: when Shackleton began shuttling supplies to Hut Point over the sea ice in August, it was all by man-hauling and using the car for the few miles of hard surface over which it would run.

In early October, David, Mawson and Mackay left Cape Royds to accomplish Ross's old dream of reaching the South Magnetic Pole, on an epic journey of their own up to the Victoria Land plateau. On 3 November, having laid an advanced depot 100 miles south, Shackleton, Adams, Marshall and Wild set off with their four surviving ponies and, until the 7th, an initial support party, to reach the South Pole. This Shackleton calculated at 747 nautical miles from Cape Royds, which he hoped would be a straight and relatively level march over the Barrier. They had 91 days food and, allowing it might be stretched to 110, this meant covering at least 12.5 miles a day. The dogs (inadequate in number) were left behind: the ponies and men without skis sank exhaustingly into the snow at every step but by 26 November they had passed the furthest south of Scott and Shackleton's first journey in 29 days, compared to 59 for Scott. By 1 December, still on the Barrier, they had only one pony left, the other three having been shot and depoted for food as they weakened. Ahead lay a line of mountains, which they could not then know were the 3,000 mile Transantarctic range, peeling off from the western side of the Ross Sea. Two days later, crossing massive pressure ridges of ice, they climbed a low pass called the Gateway and discovered beyond it their cause – the vast, rising sweep of what Shackleton was later to name the Beardmore Glacier,

The ascent of Mount Erebus; on the edge of a crater.

flowing down from the polar plateau. It was one of the few ways up to it through the mountains and had hazards of its own. This was quickly clear when their last pony vanished through a snow-bridge into one of the glacier's hundreds of hidden crevasses, itself shocking enough but also depriving them of its meat. By Christmas Day they were 9,500 feet up at the top, 550 miles from home and with about 250 to go to the Pole. They had less than a month's supplies left, their average speed was down to 9.5 miles a day against the still rising and difficult ground, continuous headwinds and blizzards that on some days stopped them leaving their tent.

By New Year's Day 1909 they were none the less closer than anyone had been to either the North or South Poles, but altitude sickness was beginning seriously to affect Shackleton in particular, as they crossed the 11,000 ft contour in temperatures of around −30°C. This they endured with inadequate clothing, having discarded as much as possible to save weight, with the result that their body temperatures (taken by Marshall) were technically below critical level. They were also increasingly malnourished. At 4am on 9 January 1909, as another blizzard died away, they left their tent and sledge to make a final dash south and plant the Union flag

that Queen Alexandra had given them at 88° 23' south. This was just 97 miles from the Pole, 360 miles further south than Scott and 730 miles from base. They had pushed their endurance to the limits and turning back was probably the bravest and hardest decision Shackleton ever made. It was better, as he later told his wife, to be a live donkey than a dead lion. Amundsen and the Norwegians fully concurred and admired him the more for it, not least because Nansen had made the same decision on his attempt to reach the North Pole in 1895. Shackleton's refusal to risk his own life and those of others beyond a certain point, and his clear judgement as to where that point lay, were among his most admirable qualities.

Having taken photographs, they immediately began the march back, now with the wind behind them and helped by a sail made from a tent floor-cloth. Their survival was dependent on following their own outward tracks and finding the small depots they had left on the way, a task made more difficult when they lost the sledgemeter wheel, which counted off the miles as they went. On 20 January, with just one day's food left and starvation threatening they found their first depot, and extra clothing, near the head of the Beardmore Glacier. At this point, even though the altitude was now decreasing rapidly, Shackleton collapsed with breathing

'Final start of the Southern Party – the Queen's flag flying ahead. Our sledge flags flying. Ponies from left to right: Socks, Grisi, Quan and Chinaman.'

'Furthest south, Queen's flag flying'. Adams, Wild and Shackleton reach the furthest point south on 9 January 1909.

difficulty and a high temperature and for some time had to be carried on the sledge. It was almost a repeat of the *Discovery* journey though without the scurvy. Fortunately the weather was good but by the time they were within a mile or so of the next depot, 40 miles on, everyone was so weak that only Marshall was able to reach it and bring back food. Finally, down on the Barrier, Shackleton recovered but the same desperate sequence was repeated, depot by depot, with dysentery added when they took meat from a pony carcass at the base of the glacier. As the last 300 miles slowly wore them down, all that saved them was generally good weather, will-power, and finally help from the party left at Cape Royds. This took the form of a large depot 50 miles south of Hut Point, which, following orders left by Shackleton, Joyce and others had laid in two journeys beginning on 15 January. For this he had at last successfully used dogs, having taken the trouble and time to form them and himself into an adequate team. Shackleton reached this point and plentiful food on 23 February but knew he had only five days left to return to Hut Point before *Nimrod*, which Joyce's note confirmed had now arrived, would sail for New Zealand giving his party up for dead. In fact this had already been assumed: they were a month overdue in terms of the food supply with which they had started. Consequently, lookouts who should have been posted for them from 25 February were not on station.

In the end, with Marshall no longer able to continue, Shackleton and

'Return of the South Party after 126 days'. Left to right: Wild, Shackleton, Marshall and Adams.

Wild made a forty-hour, 30-mile forced march practically without food and only brief rest to the *Discovery* hut, arriving on the evening of 28 February. It, too, was unexpectedly deserted and unsupplied, with an ominous note from David saying everyone else was safe but implying *Nimrod* had already sailed that day. Despair loomed until the following morning, 1 March, when the ship, now commanded by Evans from the *Koonya*, returned from a safer offing to land a small wintering party under Mawson. This had been hastily arranged after much argument on board, the sole purpose being to search for the bodies of the southern party. Astonishingly, Shackleton – who had not slept properly for over fifty hours – himself insisted on immediately leading the rescue of Marshall and Adams, a further two-day, 60-mile march out and back on foot, since the dogs were waiting for collection at Cape Royds. From this they returned on 3 March 1909, when he immediately ordered *Nimrod*'s departure for New Zealand, abandoning part of their baggage and equipment ashore rather than add a further day's risk of being trapped in the gathering ice of the southern winter.

White Warfare

Captain Robert Falcon Scott; a formal portrait photograph by Maull & Fox.

'A period of badly strained optimism' was how H.G. Wells described the opening years of the twentieth century. While predicting a world of aeroplanes, air-conditioning and cosy suburban living, he also foresaw wars more widespread than the conflict with the Boers in which Britain was engaged as 1900 began. No one was yet quite sure who the enemy would be. Some newspapers warned that the French might launch a combined forces raid on London while Britain was distracted in South Africa. Later, as the Germans began to build a navy to rival Britain's dreadnoughts, they became the more likely enemy.

Much to the glee of Britain's rivals, the war in South Africa had not gone well initially. There were major defeats at Spion Kop and elsewhere. Robert Baden-Powell and his men were besieged in Mafeking and were only relieved with much difficulty. Nevertheless the mad rejoicing in the streets at the relief brought a new word into the vocabulary, to 'maffick': - 'Mother may I go and maffick, rush around and hinder traffic?' went one rhyme, not without irony. But this could not mask fears that modern Britons were becoming decadent compared with their forebears. Baden-Powell – soon to found the Boy Scouts and already an instant hero for his role in the siege – saw disturbing parallels with the decadence and decline of the Roman empire. He warned of the dangers of physical degeneracy. He recalled how the Romans had come to grief because their soldiers 'fell away from the standard of their forefathers in bodily strength'.

Such self-doubt and uncertainty fuelled a hunger for heroes as tangible reaffirmation of Britain's greatness. But these heroes must not be swaggering, bragging types. Britain's dignity had long demanded understated, modest, self-deprecating heroes, unfailingly cheerful in the face of adversity. When Livingstone was buried in Westminster Abbey in 1874, the press lauded 'the brave, modest, self-sacrificing African explorer', enthusing that such virtues were those 'which our country has always been ready to acknowledge, which our religion has taught us to revere, and seek to cultivate and conserve'. Baden-Powell himself seemed to embody the stiff upper lip, sending laconic telegrams from Mafeking such as: 'All well. Four hours bombardment. One dog killed.' So keen were the myth makers to reinforce this image that they even claimed Baden-Powell never cried during childhood.

Edwardians thought that men should behave heroically for King, country and comrades, not out of personal ambition. Also, while winning was important, it was not everything. The good sport and the plucky loser were held in huge esteem. Although Britain topped the medals table with fifty-six gold medals at the 1908 Olympic Games at London's White City, some of the loudest applause greeted Queen Alexandra's presentation of a consolation gold cup to the Italian marathon runner Durando Pietri. He had collapsed while leading in the final lap and been disqualified for receiving help over the finishing line. In one of the rowing events at Henley, the British team chivalrously waited for their Dutch opponents to resume rowing after they had run their boat into the bank.

The ideal hero in a society steeped in the works of G.A. Henty, Rudyard Kipling and Conan Doyle also embodied a certain boyish, schoolboy fervour. J.M. Barrie, creator of Peter Pan and friend of Captain Scott, captured this somewhat naive spirit in his introduction to 'Like English gentlemen', an allegorical tribute written after Scott's death: 'And so this hero of heroes said, I am going to find the South Pole. It will be a big adventure.'

Antarctic exploration indeed seemed a 'big adventure' to the Edwardians, satisfying a number of needs in this society in transition. Firstly, national pride and precedence required that Britain should claim the South Pole. The British had long been pre-eminent in Antarctic discovery, from the days of Captain Cook to James Clark Ross and beyond. Yet, at a deeper, psychological level, Antarctica represented an ultimate testing ground, a kind of quest for the Holy Grail, where Britons could demonstrate that they retained the manly attributes of old. Sir Clements Markham, the driving force behind the 1901–04 *Discovery* expedition, fostered such thoughts, designing sledge flags like medieval pennants for the participants.

Antarctica's almost mystical remoteness was another factor. Like Barrie's 'Never Never Land', this place of mists and legends could not be seen by ordinary mortals. When Scott, Shackleton and the rest set off in 1901, it was to disappear behind an icy screen into *terra incognita* - a white, featureless wasteland. There had been many recent developments in communications. Telegraphs enabled Queen Victoria in 1897 to broadcast her message to the Empire at the single press of a button in Buckingham Palace and for it to pass through Tehran within two minutes on its way to the farthest corners of her dominions. However, all such innovations were intriguingly and entirely irrelevant in Antarctica. Once the explorers had sailed over the southern horizon the world could know nothing of their struggles and achievements until they, or a relief ship, emerged with news the following season.

Public interest in Antarctica was initially quite low-key. However, the popular press, like the *Daily Mail* – launched in 1896 priced at half a penny and with a circulation by 1900 of a million copies a day – had an appetite for heroes and new–found lands, and played an influential role. When the *Discovery* expedition was announced, the paper emphasized the quest for the Pole, rather than the scientific aspects, *The Morning Post* rejoiced: 'Even in the last throes of an exhausting struggle [the Boer War], we can yet spare the energy and the men to add to the triumphs we have already won in the peaceful but heroic field of exploration.'

They brought their readers the subsequent, joyful news that Scott, Shackleton and Wilson had reached within 400 miles of the Pole. When Sir Clements Markham, who feared a repeat of the Franklin tragedy, expressed fears for the men's safety, the papers fuelled the public's anxiety. Would the men of the *Discovery* return safely? If so, would they be emaciated, exhausted skeletons, harrowed by unimaginable experiences? When the *Discovery* finally sailed into Portsmouth Harbour in September 1904 a surprised *Daily Express* journalist reassured his readers not only that the men looked like 'seasoned mahogany' but that, against all the odds, they had positively flourished.

The press alighted on Scott who discovered, somewhat to his dismay, that he had become a 'celebrity'. His remarks to journalists that the men of the *Discovery* had been very well able to take care of themselves and had had no need of the relief vessel sent to find him endeared him to the public. Heroes were supposed to be self-sufficient, scornful of danger and disdainful of fuss. Scott was lionized by London society and invited to Balmoral by King Edward VII to report in person. He was made a CVO, although he did not receive the rumoured knighthood. An *Antarctic Exhibition* staged by Markham at London's Bruton galleries, which included several hundred of Edward Wilson's inspirational drawings, a model of the *Discovery* and sledging equipment, drew 10,000 fascinated visitors. The fashionable world descended from their carriages, horseless or otherwise, to be told by the patient policemen that they would have to queue like everyone else. It was a new experience for them to have to wait their turn and perhaps a sign of the changing times. The exhibition's photographs of the *Discovery* trapped in the ice brought the scale, magic and danger of Antarctica home to people with a compelling immediacy. They were confronted by images of a world that until then had only existed in their imagination.

Scott's lyrical account, *The Voyage of the Discovery* immediately sold out. The sentiments he expressed seemed a perfect rebuttal of all those fears about British decadence and decline. He scorned the use of dogs asserting that the only truly 'manly' way was to pull the sledge yourself. He wrote: 'No journey ever made with dogs can approach the height of that fine conception ... when men go forth ... with their own unaided efforts and ... succeed in solving some problems of the great unknown.' His philosophy was perfectly attuned to the ethos of his age. It is embodied in most Antarctic expeditions today.

What the public could not know was the personal impact the experience had had on their new hero. Scott was a fine writer and his book captured the siren beauty of Antarctica; but he could not reveal his personal feelings, the self-doubt and anxiety that had, on occasions, tormented him. A man of his time, he would have found it unthinkable to confess publicly to his lack of confidence and bouts of introspection, and it was certainly not what the public wanted from its hero. Yet, as he later confided in his wife Kathleen, Antarctica had been a personal proving ground where he had battled as much against personal weaknesses as against the bitter physical conditions.

At the same time, like Shackleton, he had fallen in love with Antarctica. They had both been attracted initially to exploration through that unheroic thing, personal ambition. Neither were well-off and both had their way to make in the world: Scott was supporting his mother and sisters, while Shackleton wanted to establish himself in the eyes of his fiancée's wealthy family. But, as they had sledged together across the Great Ice Barrier, ambition had fused with something else. Both had been gripped by Antarctica's astonishing beauty. Both had seen the possibilities it

'A British Hero'; souvenir postcard commemorating Scott, published after his death.

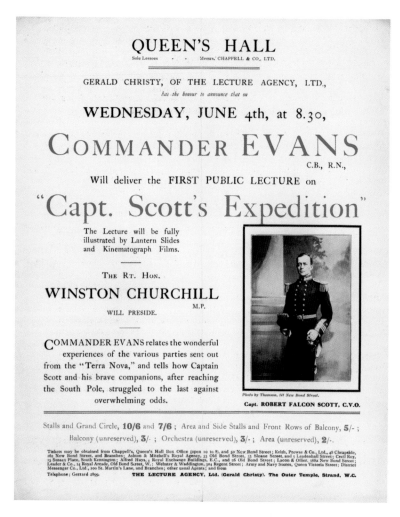

Poster advertising the first public lecture on the *Terra Nova* expedition, given by Commander 'Teddy' Evans on 4 June 1913.

offered. Both felt compelled to return by what Shackleton termed the 'Call of the South', a kind of magnetic attraction.

Both also derived some wrong messages from their experiences. If either had been less insularly British, they would have realized from Norwegian experience that the failures of their dogs resulted partly from their own failures as dog-handlers. They would have relied mainly on dogs in their further expeditions and Shackleton would probably have been first to the Pole in 1909. Also, Scott and Shackleton's strong and very different personalities and the competitive tensions between them fuelled a strong personal rivalry.

But, of course, this rivalry could not be aired in public. The attainment of the South Pole must be first and foremost for Britain's glory. When, in 1907, Shackleton announced his *Nimrod* expedition, Scott was angry at what he saw as trespassing on his territory, but his terse correspondence with Shackleton remained strictly private. All the public knew was that yet another British venture was underway. Shackleton's subsequent return in

1909, after sledging to within 97 miles of the Pole, was greeted with rapture and, within a few months, a knighthood. Shackleton was more comfortable with fame than Scott and relished courting the public. In articles about 'How I made for the South Pole' he charmed his readers with light-hearted tales of how the extreme cold had fuelled his passion for sweet puddings and how the explorers painted their hut with scenes of blazing fires and of Joan of Arc being burned to a crisp to 'convey at least an imagination of warmth'.

A master of public relations, he underplayed the drama of his experiences and this was approvingly noted. One paper proclaimed that:

> It is well that popular triumph should be accorded to other than military heroes. Lieutenant Shackleton and his companions have been the lions of the month, and never did a lion roar more modestly and more becomingly than the gallant hero, who in his speeches has shown a fund of dry humour not usually found among such men.

A postcard produced to celebrate the success of the *Nimrod* expedition.

Another rejoiced:

> 'We seem to be living in times when men have reverted to the age of the elemental heroes.'

Shackleton's decision to turn back, when so close to the Pole, was seen, in itself, as courageous. The *Dublin Express* commented that

> 'it is a brave thing to turn back.'

Lacking Scott's literary application, Shackleton employed a ghost writer to help him produce *The Heart of the Antarctic*, which was published to critical acclaim. One journal exulted: 'What may be done with a free hand by a man full of ability and confidence has been demonstrated this year by E.H. Shackleton.' It went on: 'He was fitted for his task by the possession of great organising power, a vivid imagination, the originality of genius in devising plans, and sufficient experience on which to base them, but not enough to make caution hamper his ambition.' In other words a hero's flair and daring mattered more than experience. It was a paean in praise of that most British phenomenon: the gifted amateur.

And it was as a gifted amateur that Scott again went South on the final, fatal *Terra Nova* expedition of 1910. Dogs were taken but not taken seriously. Many of Scott's colleagues were expert scientists but not one was an expert explorer. Two of the four men he was to take to the South Pole – Captain 'Titus' Oates and 'Birdie' Bowers – had never set foot on Antarctica before but had applied to join the expedition because it promised adventure. The other two, Edward Wilson and Edgar Evans, had been with Scott on the *Discovery* and had no more experience than their leader to whom they felt great loyalty.

Scott's team contrasted starkly with Amundsen and his men. The Norwegian had chosen exploration as a career, cutting his teeth on the Gerlache expedition, and was a focused 'professional' experienced in travel

Scott in tropical whites, heading south on the *Terra Nova*.

over snow and ice in the Arctic, and an expert skier and handler of dogs. From the moment Scott received the telegram from Amundsen informing him that he, too, was going south, Scott knew inwardly that the Norwegian might well beat him and this took a psychological toll. Yet publicly he had to preserve the good sportsmanship and coolness the public expected. Media 'hype' had prepared the public for a British victory despite Amundsen's late intervention. Questioned by a journalist about his chances, Scott made the nonchalant response: 'We may get through, we may not. We may have accidents to some of our transports, to the sledges or to the animals. We may lose our lives. We may be wiped out. It is all a question that lies with providence and luck.' On the surface Scott had to appear cheerful and, above all, sporting. This was, after all, the era of good sports, the luck of the game and plucky losers.

And Scott was soon to be cast as the archetypal 'plucky loser'. The news that Scott had reached the Pole only to find himself beaten by Amundsen and to perish on the return prompted an immense national outpouring of grief on a scale comparable to the reaction to the death of Diana, Princess of Wales in 1997. Headlines like 'Eight days of starvation', 'His dying Appeal to England' and 'Homage to Heroes' held the country in thrall.

The poignant photographs of the exhausted, downcast party at the Pole gave their tragedy a terrible immediacy. But it was above all Scott's letters and diaries, written in pencil because ink would have frozen, and found beneath his body, that fuelled the grief and sense of loss. If their bodies, books, letters and photographic film had not been found, the impact would have been much less. They gave substance to the heroic image. People could relive, day by day, through his eyes, a truly epic tale of men battling bravely against ever-increasing odds; selflessly caring for their starving, frost-bitten comrades; dragging their geological specimens with them until the end out of duty and pride but eventually succumbing in that blizzard-whipped green tent just a few miles from a depot of supplies that might have saved them. He wrote of colleagues who were 'unendingly cheerful' although they knew they were doomed. Scott's understated, carefully chosen words resonated and formed an elegiac and heroic epitaph: 'Had we lived, I should have had a tale to tell... which would have stirred the heart of every Englishman.'

Of course, his tale did stir hearts. In particular his account of Oates's death caused a collective lump in the throat and huge national pride. Here was a man who, rather than put his friends at risk, walked out into a blizzard to die with the briefest of comments: 'I am just going outside and may be some time.' It was the quintessential ideal of a British officer and gentleman – unsentimental, unselfpitying, self-sacrificing. The *Daily Mail* lauded the 'immortal chivalry of Captain Oates'. His former army comrades were quick to write articles recalling his gritty valour during the Boer War, which had won him the nick-name 'No Surrender Oates'. Ironically,

Scott and Kathleen at Cape Town, South Africa, *en route* to New Zealand and Scott's final departure in the *Terra Nova* for Antarctica.

The cover of the *Daily Mirror*, showing the cairn built over the bodies of Scott and his companions by Atkinson's party in November 1912.

the re-opening of his old Boer War wound, one of the effects of scurvy, was probably a major contributor to his death.

Oates's real thoughts and feelings can only be guessed. During the dark Antarctic winter at Cape Evans he had told his comrades that anyone whose weakness was jeopardizing other members of the team had a duty to shoot himself. His last letters betray a passionate attachment to life and longing for home. Yet tortured by frostbite and denied his wish to die in his sleep he had indeed contemplated suicide. His thoughts and feelings on the day he walked to his death were more complex than the public perception of simplistic heroics. Each reader must decide how much irony to read into those famous farewell words.

Similarly the image of Scott that crystallized in the popular imagination was simplistic. His earlier letters to his wife Kathleen reveal his real self. It was only to her that he had felt safe to confide his dislike of the Navy and the rigidity that his creative, dreaming side had found so stifling:

> Knock a few shackles off me, you find as great a vagabond as you ... I shall never fit in my round hole. The part of a machine has got to fit - yet how I hate it sometimes ... I love the open air, the trees, the fields and the seas, the open spaces of life and thought.

But private doubts had no place in a heroic tale. Just as Scott had

Kathleen Scott.

concealed his true feelings in life, so they were suppressed after his death. Kathleen learned of her husband's death while she sailed south to New Zealand for what should have been their reunion. In deep despair she opened her diary and confided her feelings. She tried to comfort herself with the hope that, before he died, 'the horror of his responsibility left him, for I think never was there a man with such a sense of responsibility and duty ...' The word 'horror' was replaced by 'weight' in the published version of the diary. The idea that Scott might have felt 'horror' at his responsibilities would have jarred with his heroic image. Just as with the human failings of Livingstone, General Gordon and Baden-Powell, his insecurities must not be revealed.

The press played a key role in Scott's metamorphosis into a national icon. They were quick to make comparisons with another recent and shocking tragedy, the sinking of the *Titanic* in April 1912, when women and children were flung into boats by men who knew themselves doomed, while the band played till the end. Papers reminded their readers that many of the British passengers had displayed the same cool courage and selfless concern for others. Even if there was increasing and uneasy acceptance of Darwin's theory that man was descended from the apes, and of Freud's emerging theories of the human psyche, Scott and his men, like the *Titanic*'s passengers, seemed to epitomize man's nobler instincts. But as one leader put it: 'Captain Scott died in more awful circumstances than the *Titanic*'.

The public were mesmerized. Thousands attended a memorial service in St Paul's. On the same day the 750,000 children of London's County Council schools were told Scott's story by their teachers. The *Daily Mirror* commented: 'What English boy or girl may not gain courage by saying "I will be brave as Captain Scott was - as he would wish me to be."' A memorial fund was flooded with far more money that Scott had managed, with much effort, to raise in sponsorship. Kathleen was given the status of a wife of a Knight Commander of the Order of the Bath on the grounds that this honour would have been bestowed on Scott had he survived. She was a talented sculptress and was commissioned to create several statues of her husband.

Tales about heroes generally require villains. Amundsen, genuinely distressed by Scott's death and needlessly tormented by the thought that he should have left supplies for him at the Pole, was tailor-made for the role. He was foreign. He was seen as an interloper. Even worse perhaps, he was a 'professional' whose tactics did not conform to the heroic 'amateur' mould. His achievements based on dogs rather than man-hauling seemed less virile and manly than Scott's. Put crudely, according to the chauvinist press he had won but he had not 'played the game'.

The grimness of World War I gave Scott's tragic expedition and Oates' self-sacrifice a further, deeper significance. Their unseen battle and ultimate death in the unsullied white wastes of Antarctica seemed com-

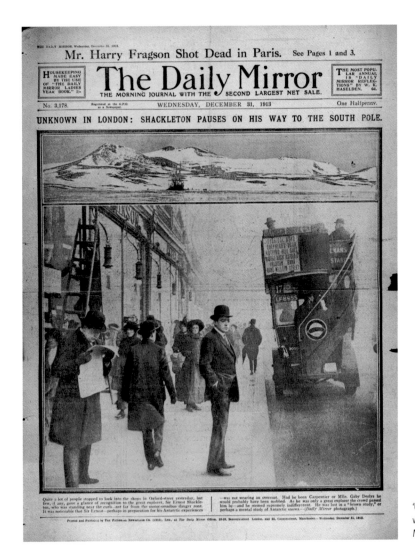

The Daily Mirror

Mr. Harry Fragson Shot Dead in Paris. See Pages 1 and 3.

No. 3,178.   WEDNESDAY, DECEMBER 31, 1913.   One Halfpenny.

UNKNOWN IN LONDON: SHACKLETON PAUSES ON HIS WAY TO THE SOUTH POLE.

'Unknown in London: Shackleton pauses on his way to the South Pole'. The cover of the *Daily Mirror*, 21 December 1913.

fortingly pure amid doubts about what the pain, mud and blood of the trenches were achieving. Shackleton's *Endurance* expedition, which set out in 1914, was similarly seized on by the press. Reports of his progress and even subsequent fears for his life were a welcome distraction from worrying news from the front. By 1915 the papers were attracting their readers' attention with such headlines as 'Bad News from the Antarctic' and 'Shackleton's Plight'. News of his survival reached Britain on the day of the Battle of Jutland. At a time when millions had already died, the public were cheered to learn that, despite appalling odds, Shackleton had not lost a single man. The news transcended national barriers: even the German press commented favourably. As with Scott's last expedition, one of the most powerful heroic images was the gradual focusing down of the story onto the leader. First Shackleton had all his men with him, then he took only five on the boat journey from Elephant Island to South Georgia.

Finally, he led just two companions over the mountains and ice of South Georgia to find help.

As generations passed, the circumstances of Scott's death and his extraordinary gift as a writer, established him rather than Shackleton, as the leading national hero until the reassessments of the 1960s and 1970s. Shackleton has now emerged alongside him as, perhaps, a more 'modern' hero – an inspirational leader with shrewd judgement and the common touch. His comment that he turned back from the Pole in 1909 out a of belief that his wife would rather be married to a live donkey than a dead lion is telling. So are some of his decisions like jettisoning the team's sleeping bags when they set out across South Georgia. He was a brilliant calculator of risk and it is easy to see why so many management consultants today use him as a case study in courses about risk and crisis management and leadership skills. He did not allow his feelings to upset his judgement, as Scott did when he decided to take four not three men with him to the Pole. Amundsen, too, seems in tune with our own time. His organizational skills, logical mind and strong focus are qualities we value and admire today. And it should not be forgotten that Amundsen was first to the Pole and that this was just one achievement in a remarkable career.

Perceptions of heroism vary across generations. What seems determination in one age can appear as obsession in another, self-sacrifice can seem self-indulgence even self-destruction, optimism becomes rashness, and bravery just foolhardiness. Scott, Shackleton and Amundsen were all three physically strong, brave and undoubted 'heroes'. However, from our perspective today we can see how part of Scott's heroism – his successful struggle to master his own weaknesses – remained hidden, Amundsen's achievement was denigrated and Shackleton's spectacular contribution for a while overshadowed. The passing of time brings greater clarity and objectivity though it can also make us more critical and suspicious of the 'heroes' of earlier times. But the story of the race for the South Pole transcends this: it has an extraordinary, universal power and rightly moves us still.

The Race to the Pole

Menu from a dinner given at the Savage Club to welcome home officers from the *Discovery* expedition, 5 November 1904. It is signed by both Scott and Shackleton among others.

Exploration of the Arctic and Antarctic in the hundred years before World War I involved similar risks and many of the same people. There was also a broad distinction between two types of expedition, irrespective of which Pole it was. The first, dominated by the British, involved largely official naval parties, heavily manned and well equipped, with a generally scientific and geographical motive. They often made arduous overland journeys largely man-hauling their sledges – which became a British orthodoxy. Some casualties usually resulted, although the loss of Franklin's expedition was exceptional. The second was the speculative hunting operations of whalers or sealers. These arrived in the Antarctic with experience of Arctic conditions and sometimes a non-commercial leavening of private scientific interest. While the Enderbys best represent the British involvement in such activities (see page 17), by the 1890s it was the Norwegians for whom it was a more significant national business. Generally this type of foray attempted little or no land travel, for obvious reasons.

In between, there were also other scientific expeditions, with or without some level of naval support. At the same time as the *Discovery* was preparing to head south, so were a German party under Professor von Drygalski, Swedish and French parties to Graham Land on the Antarctic Peninsula, under Dr Otto Nordenskjöld and Dr J.B. Charcot respectively, and another to the Weddell Sea under the experienced Scottish naturalist and explorer, Dr William S. Bruce. While both the *Discovery* and *Nimrod* expeditions fell into this bracket the former was Royal Naval in its approach, scale and methods, whereas the latter had much in common with de Gerlache's equally hand-to-mouth and romantically motivated *Belgica* venture (see page 19), though it achieved much more.

Scott represents the end of a long tradition of Royal Naval officers who took up polar exploration primarily as a means of advancing their careers and he might have retired as an admiral had he not died as a result. Albeit not a commercial voyager in the whalers' sense, Shackleton was no less a career seaman seeking the rewards of enterprise – though he showed no gift for accumulating fortune. He, too, went to the Antarctic by chance, caught the polar 'bug' and aimed to exploit his success as an explorer financially and for new projects as an early example of a 'media celebrity'. His personality and presentational skills were much more suited to this than either Amundsen's or Scott's (though Scott was the best writer), and the fact he was knighted on his return in 1909 was partly a recognition of his success as a public figure as well as his achievements as an explorer. The acclaim with which his 'near-miss' at the South Pole was greeted – in the year that also saw the North reached – put polar exploration back on the British public agenda.

Neither Scott nor Shackleton came from a 'cold-climate' background, a disadvantage on both a personal and technical level. More insidious was the varying degree to which they took the superiority of established British naval methods for granted, superficially absorbing foreign equipment improvements but not the underlying advances in approach. The insular aversion to using sledge-dogs was a prime example, compounded by the error of substituting horses without well-proved reason. Shackleton at least learnt that these were mistakes, though only fully so after Amundsen's success: Scott repeated them and paid a heavy price. It is however ironic that he and Shackleton – not Amundsen – saw that the future lay with motorized transport, ineffective as their pioneering attempts to use it were.

As a Norwegian, Amundsen came from a different tradition and a country that around 1900 had a population of under two million, one tenth of Britain's. Here individualistic merchant seafaring and whaling,

Fram
1910–12

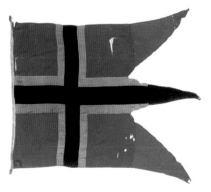

Amundsen and his dog Rex, in his garden at Bundefjord, in the summer of 1910, with *Fram* in the background.

One of the Norwegian flags taken to the Pole by Amundsen. 2.5m x 1.5m, 8ft x 5ft (approx)

untainted by British social contempt for 'trade', were a dominant commercial expression of a sub-arctic climate and a circumscribed, clannish, non-industrial and certainly non-imperial society. No less patriotic than Scott or Shackleton, Amundsen had a very different and modern example before him. This was Dr Fridjtof Nansen, who had shown how someone from such a culture might become a figure of world repute through Arctic discovery and thereby enhance the prestige of their small nation. From the beginning Amundsen made this his goal, by becoming a professional polar explorer in a way that Scott, Shackleton and most of their forebears were not. His success lay in methodical analysis and adoption of relevant experience and skills from whatever source, meticulous planning and a reliance on hand-picked small teams rather than large, heterogeneous and heavily resourced parties.

Roald Amundsen was born on 16 July 1872 near Christiania, which became Norway's capital, Oslo, after her independence from Sweden in 1905. He grew up on the forested edge of the city but spent much of his childhood alongside his cousins on their adjoining country homes near the port of Sarpsborg. His father and uncles were shipowners and masters there, though his father died when he was fourteen, in 1886. The following

A model of *Fram* with a detail of the protective awnings Amundsen had made to protect his dogs, primarily from the Sun.

year he was enthralled by Sir John Franklin's accounts of his overland expeditions of 1819–22 and 1825–27 in the North American Arctic and in 1888 was even more inspired by the Norwegian first crossing of the Greenland ice cap. This was led by Nansen – a marine biologist and already an explorer of note – and laid the foundations of Norway's success in polar discovery, using a small, lightly equipped and fast-moving party, on skis and with much improved sledges of Nansen's design. (Scott took Nansen sledges on both the *Discovery* and *Terra Nova* expeditions.) Thereafter Amundsen devoted himself to energetic improvement of his own skiing, including arduous and, later, risky treks in Norway. Like Shackleton, he was a poor scholar but on matriculation in 1890 followed his mother's wishes and began to train as a doctor. Exploration, however, strengthened its hold on his interests. In February 1893 he attended a lecture by Eivind Astrup, who had been with the indefatigable American, Robert Peary, on his second Greenland expedition in 1891-92, and who recounted their experience of learning polar techiques from the Eskimos, especially driving sledge-dogs and building igloos. The use of dogs was itself then barely known in Norway and the idea that 'primitives' like the Eskimo might have something to teach Europeans was also novel. Amundsen, however, had an open and retentive mind and a great capacity to grasp and build on essentials.

His future crystallized that year. Early in June he failed his exams, just before seeing Nansen in his new ship, *Fram* ('Forward'), sail on his greatest expedition to drift with the pack-ice across the Arctic Ocean and make an epic sledge assault on the North Pole. Soon afterwards, in September 1893, Amundsen lost his mother. They had not been close and, with a useful inheritance, he abandoned medicine to pursue his own directions. He immediately attempted to join a Norwegian expedition to Spitsbergen and made enquiries about the British one under Jackson to Franz Josef Land. The latter expedition was to be Nansen's fortuitous salvation when he miraculously emerged on foot in Franz Josef Land in 1896, being fortunate in finding the Jackson-Harmsworth expedition there. The *Fram* reappeared independently and equally unscathed in Norway a week after him. Amundsen's applications came to nothing but showed that he recognized the essential requirements. Over the next few years he became both an experienced mountain skier and a seaman, through embarking on a series of voyages in sealers. In 1895 he gained his mate's certificate and the following year volunteered to be unpaid second mate on de Gerlache's private Belgian Antarctic expedition in the *Belgica*. This sailed in June 1897 and after its long imprisonment in the southern ice only returned in 1899. It was a voyage on which Amundsen learnt a great deal about the behaviour of men under prolonged stress and more about Greenland Eskimo practice. The voyage's American doctor, Frederick Cook, had been with Peary in Greenland. He and Amundsen found common interests in perfecting equipment and techniques, while others (including de

Gerlache) became depressed and in some cases insane under the constant threat that the ship – an old sealer – would be crushed beneath them. Cook was also a believer in the power of fresh meat to ward off scurvy, a point proved when one man died from the disease after refusing to eat seal or penguin.

On return home Amundsen went back to sea to earn a master's certificate and in 1900 bought the 47-ton sloop *Gjøa* with which he made a sealing voyage to the Barents Sea to gain experience in polar navigation. He had then already formed a plan to be the first man to sail completely through the North-West Passage and re-establish the shifting position of the North Magnetic Pole – having also learnt that a scientific rationale was the only way to gain financial backing for exploration. In fact, for technical reasons, he missed the Magnetic Pole by 30 miles but the transit of the Passage with a party of six in the *Gjøa*, which took from 1903 to 1906, was otherwise a triumphant success. In particular, he established good relations with the Eskimos and gained a huge amount of knowledge from them about everything polar, from the virtues of native fur clothing to the building of igloos and the driving of sledge dogs. In this one of his seaman companions, Helmer Hanssen, became extremely expert. The long voyage also established him as a successful leader and a figure to be reckoned with internationally in the polar field.

Example of a wolfskin jacket of Inuit (Netsilik) design, used by the Norwegian team on the *Fram* expedition.

In February 1907 Amundsen was at the Royal Geographical Society in London with Nansen, as Norway's resident Minister there, to lecture on the *Gjøa* voyage. Shackleton was also present on his own business. He had just secured Beardmore's backing for the *Nimrod* voyage, which was announced the next day, and was about to find out that Scott was already thinking of a new Antarctic voyage.

Amundsen himself had also come to London to ask Nansen for the loan of *Fram* for a new expedition. The American, Peary, had so far failed to reach the North Pole on several land-based attempts. Amundsen's aim now, starting in 1910, was to pass through the Bering Strait from San Franciso and drift for four or five years with the ice as Nansen had done, with the aim of being the first there. Nansen eventually agreed and, though fundraising proved a major difficulty, all was progressing when in early September 1909 news broke that both Cook – Amundsen's old shipmate – and then Peary (on his sixth attempt) had independently achieved the North Pole. The former claimed to have done so in April 1908, the latter on 6 April 1909. Peary immediately challenged Cook's claim, which was later discounted, though his own has also been doubted.

For Amundsen, however, it did not matter: he would not be the first and that left only one course. By the time Scott's proposal for what would be his last expedition was announced in *The Times* on 13 September 1909, Amundsen had already visited Copenhagen, ostensibly to meet Cook, but also to order sufficient dogs and Eskimo furs there from northern Green-land, with the South Pole now his prime objective. Given that all his backing, including from the Norwegian government, was for a northern voyage he told no one of his change of plan, including those who sailed with him, until it was unavoidable. When he finally announced his intentions from Madeira, *Fram*'s last port-of-call before the Ross Sea, he

The telegram sent to Scott in Melbourne, informing him of Amundsen's decision to turn south, 5 October 1910.

also explained the change as an addition rather than an alternative to his northern project. *Fram* had to sail round Cape Horn to Alaska and his South Polar assault was to be a diversion on the way. As for Scott, when he had visited Norway in March 1910 and sought a meeting, Amundsen deliberately avoided him: they never met in person.

Amundsen sailed in *Fram* on 9 August 1910 from Kristiansand, after an extensive Atlantic work-up cruise, with ninety-seven top-class Eskimo dogs and two expert Norwegian drivers among his crew, one being Hansson. Every detail of his programme, equipment and supplies had been minutely prepared for the expected conditions and nearly all his men were individually recruited for relevant skills and their ability to operate as a team under his unquestioned leadership. His intention was to set up a base where he and nine men could winter, on the Barrier in Shackleton's Bay of Whales, sending *Fram* away on an oceanographic cruise based on Buenos Aires. Most would then make a rapid, depot-based, dog and ski march to the Pole at the end of 1911. All would be collected again early in 1912 to head for the Arctic though, unsurprisingly perhaps, Amundsen first delayed and then never did fulfil his original northern plan.

The first Scott was to hear of this was on 13 October 1910, in Melbourne, where his new expedition had just arrived. Amundsen had overestimated the interest the British press would show in his change of direction: it passed little noticed, as too incredible to be taken seriously. Consequently nothing had been reported in Australia to explain the cryptic telegram Scott received there from Amundsen's brother, Leon: 'Beg leave to inform you *Fram* proceeding Antarctic. Amundsen.' The Norwegians had started their voyage two months after Scott but that was his sole advantage.

> 'I don't hold that anyone but an Englishman should get to the S. Pole.'
>
> Scott to Sir Arthur Moore, 21 September 1909

> 'It is sad we have been forestalled by the Norwegians, but I am glad that we have done it by good British man-haulage. That is the traditional British sledging method...'
>
> Henry Bowers, at the Pole, 17 January 1912

Scott's return from the south in September 1904 saw his advancement both to captain and Companion of the Royal Victorian Order. His publication of *The Voyage of the Discovery* in 1905 was also a literary and financial success, although criticism of the expedition's home organization, costs, and some of its scientific results cast various shadows in official quarters. Overall it established Scott as a public figure but its achievements were specialized and, taken with his lack of colour, did not produce the sustained popular enthusiasm that later greeted Shackleton.

In an era of rapid naval advance Scott's long absence had also rendered him inexperienced for the rank he now held. Despite some promising short-term battleship commands (one involving a minor collision for which he was not blamed but might have avoided), his outlook was not overly promising by the time he took up a staff job under the Second Sea Lord in 1909.

By 1906, however, he was again contemplating the tonic of Antarctic achievement, hence his exaction of Shackleton's promise not to stray onto what he considered 'his' territory, the Victoria Land side of the Ross Sea. He wisely said nothing to the Navy but gained the private help of Lieutenant Michael Barne from *Discovery*, whose own proposal for a Weddell Sea party had just withered under the disapproval of the First Lord, Admiral Fisher. Lieutenant 'Teddy' Evans also volunteered to join him again and he recruited his *Discovery* engineer, Commander Skelton, who put in a huge amount of work to develop a tracked motor-sledge unit. It was on this idea of Skelton's, aired in *Discovery* and for which Barne helped to obtain backing, that Scott now pinned his hopes of reaching the Pole. The rationale was to be technical as well as scientific.

Markham was still influential, though no longer in power at the RGS, and Scott's other major ally was his new wife. Kathleen Bruce, then rising thirty, was a talented sculptress with emancipated views and a bohemian lifestyle, whom he met in early 1906 through his sister, Ettie Ellison-Macartney. She was more worldly and outwardly confident than Scott, but she none the less came to regard him as the hero she sought to be the father of her son and his success became her mission: he in turn idolized her and found in her a *confidante* for all his uncertainties. She was handsome, charismatic and well-connected, including with senior naval men. They married on 2 September 1908 and were soon expecting their only

'View of the Grotto Berg with Taylor in the foreground', taken by Herbert Ponting, 8 January 1911.

'Crean, Taylor and Wright in the Main-top of the *Terra Nova*, looking over the ice-pack', 22 December 1910.

son Peter, born on 14 September 1909. In between, Scott's last staff appointment was obtained partly through her social contacts and he took it up on 24 March. It was the same day that he heard Shackleton had – so dishonourably in his view – reached within 100 miles of the South Pole.

In September 1909, with Shackleton's success boosting British public interest, came the news of Cook and Peary's claims to have reached the North Pole. German and Japanese expeditions south were also in prospect and on the 13th – almost exactly when Amundsen suddenly switched his 'polarity' – Scott announced he would head south in 1910. 'The main object of the expedition', he wrote, 'is to reach the South Pole and secure for the British Empire the honour of this achievement'. Shackleton's own immediate plans to return came to nothing but he assured Scott there would be no clash of interests.

Scott's preparations this time combined aspects of both the *Discovery* and *Nimrod* voyages. Again there was a naval backbone but he had to raise the funding himself, eventually around £50,000. He shortened his deadline of August to 1 June 1910, to fit the southern seasons, thus giving him nine months rather than Shackleton's seven (let alone Amundsen's or *Discovery*'s two years). It was a formidable task, the final money only being found in Australia and New Zealand, but there was patriotic home support from sponsors, who gave supplies and equipment, contributions from schools for dogs and horses, and a £20,000 grant from the government.

Discovery was unavailable, having been sold to the Hudson's Bay Company. He instead chose the old *Terra Nova*, the 700-ton Scottish steam-auxiliary whaler built in 1884, which the Admiralty had sent to rescue him in 1904 and had then resold for whaling. She was in a run-down state and Evans did wonders converting her but the conditions on board were to be as crowded, overloaded, unpleasant and dangerous as in

Oates with some of the ponies in the *Terra Nova*.

Nimrod. She nearly foundered in a Southern Ocean storm before reaching McMurdo Sound due to failure to renew her emergency pump and the fact that, after New Zealand, she had no engineer officer. Because Skelton outranked him, albeit as a specialist engineer, Evans did not want him on board: Scott had to choose and ditched Skelton. It was not the first time he had used people then changed horses and in the light of events this was probably a mistake.

Edward Wilson, Scott's indispensable support, had long agreed to come as artist and head of the strong scientific staff, which included Raymond Priestley the geologist from *Nimrod,* who was picked up in New Zealand. Other *Discovery* hands included Crean, Lashly and the burly Welsh petty officer, Edgar Evans. Scott was also besieged by some 8,000 volunteers of all sorts. Markham played a hand in his agreement to take the Royal Indian Marine lieutenant, the humorous Scot, Henry Bowers, known as 'Birdie' for his aquiline features. Money also talked. The well-off but unpretentiously spartan cavalryman, Captain Lawrence Oates of the 6th Inniskilling Dragoons, had been badly wounded in the Boer War. Bored with peacetime service, he volunteered, offering £1,000 for a place. Ignoring the lesson of Shackleton's experience, Scott intended to take Manchurian ponies for his polar trek. Since Oates knew a great deal about horses he got his berth but what Scott then failed to do was to send him to buy them. This was left to Cecil Meares, a rather mysterious Russian expert, reputedly with spying connections, and the only experienced British dog driver to be taken. Nansen had prevailed on Scott to include

A sample page from an issue of the *South Polar Times*, showing Wilson's skills as a wildlife artist and illustrator.

some dogs, despite his lack of faith in them, and Meares made an epic journey of his own to Siberia to buy thirty-three good ones, a third of those taken by Amundsen. In addition he was almost casually told to pick up some ponies as well, though he knew nothing about them. Oates immedi-

Group in the wardroom of the *Terra Nova*.

ately saw that the twenty he shipped 8,000 miles from Mukden to New Zealand were over-priced 'crocks': one died *en route*. A Russian dog driver and Russian groom were also to be taken south by Scott.

He took the same attitude to skis as to dogs: despite having tried them on the *Discovery* voyage, he had never seen *effective* skiing until he visited Norway for a less than exhaustive test of a sledge tractor. Here Nansen introduced him to Tryggve Gran, a wealthy young Norwegian who had been trying to mount his own southern expedition. Gran's competent skiing so impressed Scott that he had a Pauline conversion, decided that skis should be taken and asked Gran to come as instructor. With today's hindsight, when thousands of far better-equipped amateurs know how difficult it is to master skiing as an adult, Scott's belief that his novices could do so as part of an expedition in which their lives might depend on it seems bizarre. (Amundsen's polar team were mostly better skiers than Gran, one – Olav Bjaaland – being a champion, and most Norwegians learnt to ski as soon as they could walk.)

Others who were to play significant roles in Scott's team were Apsley Cherry-Garrard, a young Cambridge graduate who also paid his way and wrote one of the best accounts of the venture; the retired naval lieutenant Victor Campbell, who was first mate and was to command a second shore party eventually landed to explore Victoria Land; and Herbert Ponting, the photographer whose stills and film footage were to immortalize Scott's last expedition in visual form. Scott became known as 'the Owner', Teddy Evans as the 'Skipper', the formidable Campbell as 'the Wicked Mate' and

Oates as 'Titus' or 'the Soldier'. Wilson, the peacemaker, was known as 'Uncle Bill'.

The ship's patriotic send-off from London on 1 June 1910 was under the Naval white ensign, Scott having been made a member of the Royal

Ensign presented to the crew of the *Terra Nova* by Lyttelton District High School, New Zealand. (1.52m x 3.25m, 5ft x 10ft 8ins)

The *Terra Nova* in the pack ice.

Yacht Squadron, which has the privilege of flying it. Kathleen Scott, Teddy Evans's wife, and Wilson's, travelled by steamer as far as New Zealand. What would be last farewells for two of them took place when *Terra Nova* sailed from Port Chalmers on 29 November. She started to unload at McMurdo Sound on 5 January 1911 after the stormy passage, on which two ponies died and one dog was swept overboard. Scott was obliged to set up his camp at Cape Evans on Ross Island, 12 miles north of Hut Point, rather than as intended at Cape Crozier, on the eastern side and closer to the Pole. During unloading one of the much-vaunted motor sledges proved too heavy for the sea-ice and was lost, falling to the bottom of the Sound.

'Planting the ice anchors'; a sketch by Wilson.

Scott, Simpson, Bowers and Evans leaving for the Western Mountains, 15 September 1911.

Scott 13 April 1911.

On 24 January Scott led out a large party to begin setting up depots south across the Barrier. Wilson and Meares successfully drove two dog teams but Scott remained sceptical about them until their good performance was reinforced by Oates's worst fears about the ponies. As with Shackleton's, they struggled through deep snow rather than trotting on top of it and alternately sweated and froze, necessitating constant care (unlike dogs, which do not sweat and have thick fur). All their feed was also additional weight to carry since Antarctica provides inexhaustible seal and penguin meat for dogs and men, nothing for herbivores. After only eighteen days march they were weakening and Oates advised driving them as far as possible before butchering them as meat depots for the Polar party. The more sentimental Scott sent three back, only one of which survived the journey. Overall the result was that when they finally laid their most southerly main supply dump, the famous 'One Ton' depot, it was only 130 miles south from Cape Evans and about 35 north of the point intended, the 80th parallel of latitude.

The party returned to Hut Point again at the end of February but not before Bowers, Cherry-Garrard and Crean made the mistake of camping on weak sea ice to the south with four of the five surviving ponies. It broke up in the night, leaving them adrift with one pony lost and killer whales in the offing. Crean leapt from floe to floe to get help from Scott on the Barrier proper, and his companions also managed to reach safety, abandoning the horses. When a chance arose to rescue them next day, two fell in the sea and had to be killed with pick-axes before the whales got them. The temporary ice break-up also marooned the whole party uncomfort-

Members of the Norwegian expedition model their individually adapted snow goggles at Framheim, winter, 1911.

Olav Bjaaland planing down sledge runners in his workshop at Framheim.

ably in the old *Discovery* hut, within sight of Cape Evans, until mid-April.

By then, in late February, Scott had learnt in a message from Campbell on *Terra Nova* that he had been unable to get ashore on King Edward VII Land on the east of the Ross Sea, as first intended. On 3 February he had instead found Amundsen setting up camp near the Barrier edge in the Bay of Whales, where *Fram* had arrived ten days after Scott and 60 miles closer to the Pole. The meeting was formally polite and hospitable on both sides, with Amundsen being quite frank about his intention to reach the Pole at the first opportunity. It was clear to Campbell that they were a compact, highly prepared, comfortably quartered group (*Fram* was luxurious compared to *Terra Nova*) and impressively fast-moving dog and ski specialists – a small display of Norwegian gamesmanship in this regard having greeted their guests' arrival. Amundsen invited Campbell to set up a base nearby but he naturally declined, hurried back to leave the news and his two ponies at Hut Point, and went on to set up a base camp near Cape Adare, before *Terra Nova* left to winter in New Zealand.

Scott recognized that it was going to be a race but not how fast the prize was slipping from him. Amundsen had setbacks with his tents, inadequate ski-boots, some personal frictions and medical problems: he himself was a martyr to serious piles, a bane of Polar life. He also over-taxed his dogs before they were re-acclimatized to polar conditions. None the less, on 14 February he laid a depot at 80° south, 35 miles beyond Scott's 'One Ton', in just four days for the outward journey from 'Framheim', as he called his base. In the first week of March, when Scott had already finished sledging for the season, the Norwegians laid their

Doorway sketch by Wilson.

Cherry-Garrard, Bowers, Oates, Meares and Atkinson in their spartan quarters, nick-named 'the Tenements'.

furthest depot at 82° south, over 150 miles beyond 'One Ton'. This caused some dissatisfaction: their target had been latitude 83°, a further 69 miles, Amundsen's philosophy being to include large margins of safety at every point. Building up seal-meat at the 80° depot on a final April journey, days before Scott at last got back to Cape Evans, they lost two dogs in a crevasse. Otherwise there were no significant problems and they were covering anything between 15 and 50 miles a day. In a series of rapid forays over two months, Amundsen's eight men and fifty dogs had moved three times the weight of supplies further than Scott had moved a ton in a single month-long march with thirteen men and eight ponies, seven of which had been lost.

Scott's party passed the winter on the *Discovery* pattern. Class distinctions were preserved, officers and men being separated in the Cape Evans hut but all busy on scientific observations, or on servicing equipment. Wilson revived the *South Polar Times*, Ponting gave magic lantern shows and Midwinter Day (Antarctic Christmas) was celebrated on 22 June. There then unfolded the story recounted by Cherry-Garrard in *The Worst Journey in the World*, when, on the 27th, Scott allowed Wilson to take him and Bowers to collect Emperor penguin eggs from the rookery at Cape Crozier, for research purposes. It was a man-hauling trip in darkness over rough terrain, dragging two heavy sledges and making no more than one or two miles a day. The temperature dropped as low as −77.5° F, clothing was inadequate and they barely escaped with their lives when their tent blew away in a blizzard. Fortunately they recovered it and staggered home in late July, badly frostbitten.

The Arctic winter night lifted in the third week of August and on 13 September Scott outlined his plans for the Pole. The march would begin with seventeen men and end with a group of four reaching it: overall it

Midwinter day dinner at Cape Evans, 22 June 1911.

Scott in his den at Cape Evans, 7 October 1911.

would be a journey of over 1,600 miles, setting out with the ponies but, once they were dead on the outward journey, man-hauling the sledges and using the tractors. These would pull supplies out ahead while the still ambivalently regarded dogs would shuttle forage up the line for the ponies and then return to base.

Not all was well, partly due to the strains of close living over a long winter: Scott's outer calm and methodical work concealed growing self-doubt about his own and the expedition's capacities, which burst out as hectoring and abusive bouts of temper. There was growing tension with his second-in-comand Teddy Evans, with whom he was now dissatisfied as a 'duffer' when not at sea. Evans was to defy Scott's assessment, becoming a war hero and later Admiral Lord Mountevans. Oates also concluded Scott was not a good leader and felt blamed for the deficiencies of the ponies.

Scott's group set out on 1 November 1911, man-hauling sledges, and reached One Ton on the 15th through unseasonable blizzard conditions. On the way they passed Evans's abandoned motor sledges which had started six days ahead: one had died 14 miles from Hut Point the other just under 50 miles. The technology had proved premature and Evans and Lashly unexpectedly had to man-haul from then on. Scott caught them up on the 21st and three days later the first pony was shot to feed the dog teams of Meares and the Russian driver, Dimitri Gerov. On the 28th, just after laying the Middle Barrier depot, the next pony was killed and the following day they passed Scott's furthest south point of 1902. The weather continued to be bad, with blizzards of snow and warmer temperatures that left them with sopping clothes and sleeping bags. When they

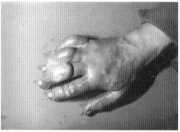

Dr Atkinson's frost-bitten hand.

Wilson, Bowers and Cherry-Garrard on their return from Cape Crozier.

pitched what they called Shambles Camp near the foot of the 110-mile ascent of the Beardmore Glacier on 9 December, the last of their ten ponies was killed. From now on they would be man-hauling their 700 lb sledges entirely themselves.

They could not know that they had already lost the race to the Pole. Amundsen had a false start on 8 September when he set out too early with seven men, Framheim being left with only his cook in charge. A week later, with both dogs and men defeated by intense cold he returned in precipitate disarray. This sparked a mutiny from two of his party, primarily Hjalmer Johansen, an experienced former companion of Nansen's who had personal problems and had been wished on him. (He was to commit suicide in 1913.) Amundsen crushed the opposition and on 15 October set off with just five men, four sledges and fifty-two dogs, leaving Johansen and the other two to mount a successful 'first-footing' on King Edward VII Land – just ahead of the Japanese as it turned out. Despite bad weather and some bad terrain he made up to 20 miles in a day of five or six hours bracing sledging, dry and warm in Eskimo furs. Dogs, sledges and skilled skiers floated over the surface, and the rest of the time both men and animals ate and rested well. Each of his sledges was carrying double the weight of supplies of Scott's. Moreover, the margins of safety already established with his depots as far as 82° south had increased with the reduction of his party. They were further reinforced beyond 82° by a change of plan in which his plentiful supplies allowed him to lay further well-marked depots at each advancing degree of latitude (that is, every 60 nautical miles). This lightened the load for his dogs and ensured no desperate marches on his return. Scott, by contrast, had assumed that the weather would be better than was occurring and had no margins of safety beyond One Ton. His man-made clothing did not match Amundsen's Eskimo furs' capacity to retain warmth and avoid sweating, and his use of skis was as little more than snow-shoes. Except for Meares, Gerov and the dogs, his men and horses trudged for eight hours a day to cover no more than 13 miles, damp and freezing by turns.

Being further east in the Ross Sea, Amundsen's journey over the Barrier was longer than Scott's, but that in the more debilitating high altitude of the Polar plateau about 120 miles shorter. By 17 November the Norwegians were off the Barrier on ground unseen by man, with the Queen Maud Range (Amundsen's name) of the Transantarctic Mountains rising up to 15,000 feet above them. A turn westward over increasingly difficult outlying ridges unexpectedly delivered them on the 19th to the edge of what Amundsen was to call the Axel Heiberg Glacier, after one of his patrons. It was an awesome sight: not the gradual 100-mile slope of the Beardmore down from the Polar plateau but a drop of 8,000 feet over 20 miles, most compressed within just eight. Amundsen took it by storm, using the remaining forty-two dogs in relays to get the sledges up, and by 21 November was on top, having covered 44 miles since leaving the Barrier in just four days.

They were only 274 miles from the Pole at a camp called 'The Butcher's Shop', for here, having praised the dogs' performance, they immediately though regretfully shot twenty-four of them according to a prearranged plan. These were fed to the surviving dogs while Amundsen and his men also ate the choicer cuts, correctly believing it would help prevent scurvy: 'Wonderful dinners we have enjoyed from our good Greenlanders and I'll say they tasted good' wrote Bjaaland. From then on it would be three sledges only. With these they worked carefully forward through a continuing series of blizzards and an area of treacherous crevasses still called the Devil's Glacier which, ironically, is now known to form the head of a less precipitous ascent (the Amundsen Glacier). By 8 December they were clear and in much improved weather passed Shackleton's furthest south of 97 miles from the Pole, saluting how well he had done.

On the same day, to the north, Scott was some 250 miles behind at the foot of the Beardmore. He had covered 379 miles in 38 days, compared to Amundsen who had at about the same stage done 385 in 29. On the 9th the last five starving and exhausted ponies were shot. Two days later, having taken them further than intended to assist the party up the lower slopes and establish the Lower Glacier Depot, Scott sent Meares, Gerov and the dogs home. Scott now knew his prejudices against dogs were a misjudgement but there were no supplies for them to go further. It was to be a hard journey on short rations, both for Meares and for the last support party who were to follow from the top of the Glacier. Between the appropriately named 'Shambles' depot of pony meat below it and 'One Ton' at 79° 28.5' south – a distance of over 400 miles – Scott had placed just two others. Amundsen by contrast had six, one at every degree of latitude back to 80° south and only a little further between the last and Framheim.

With the dogs gone, the British party was man-hauling alone on a slope up to nearly 9,000 feet. This meant 200 lb a man on their waist-harnesses, the sledges having to be painfully jerked free as they caught in deep snow or because their runners froze rapidly to the surface. With all the ponies gone too, this was the price of Scott's 'fine conception' of facing 'hardships, dangers and difficulties with their own unaided efforts'. Bowers, who had welcomed the idea of man-haulage as a 'fine-thing' that would disprove 'the supposed decadence of the British race' now found it 'the most backbreaking work I have ever come up against'. Scott had found by experience that, however inexpert their use of skis was, they greatly increased safety over crevassed areas. Sometimes using them, and some-times not, he set a tiring pace to improve on Shackleton's timings. Near the top of the glacier the first four of the support party, including the surgeon Edward Atkinson and Cherry-Garrard, were sent back leaving just two sledges to go on. Scott's was pulled by himself, Wilson, Oates and Petty Officer Evans. The other team was led by Bowers, with the tough seamen Lashly and Crean, and Lieutenant Teddy Evans. The last Scott now treated with ill-concealed hostility, overlooking that he and Lashly had been man-hauling 400 miles further than the others since the motors broke down. On Christmas Day Bowers's team was nearly lost in a cre-vasse, into which Lashly fell to the full length of his harness, while making an uphill march of over 14 miles. The increasingly worn-down party was being driven as much as led.

Amundsen's sledging compass, with the date of his arrival at the Pole carved on it. (height: 95mm 3¾ins, length: 135mm 5¼ins)

On New Year's Eve, to save weight but also precluding debate over who would go to the Pole, Scott ordered Bowers's team to depot their skis and continue on foot. On 3 January, now up on the plateau and 150 miles from the Pole, he confirmed his own group as the 'Southern Party' but at the last minute added Bowers. At the same time he ignored the medical opinion of both Wilson and Atkinson that Lashly and Crean were fitter than PO Evans, who had also badly cut his hand adjusting the sledges. Oates's work with the horses was done, he was visibly tiring and limping from his war-wounded leg, and he was already having trouble with his feet. None the less, Scott did not question his fitness to go on, wanting a representative of the army as well as of the lower deck at the Pole. A more perceptive man would have seen that it was honour and iron self-control that kept Oates going and it would have been a kindness to send him back. The reasons for taking Bowers were that he was the only reliable navigator after Teddy Evans, loyal to Scott and immensely strong. However, being short-legged compared to the others and now (by Scott's order) without skis, he was at a disadvantage for sledge-hauling, while an extra man in the four-man tent added to the discomfort of all. Even worse, the supplies for the last lap were calculated on only four and the addition of a fifth, albeit adding his rations, threw apportionment and fuel issues out of kilter. The Southern Party in fact set out on a diet of some 4,500 calories a day for an

Scott's snow goggles, recovered from his tent in November 1912.

The Southern Party on the Polar plateau; a photograph taken by 'Birdie' Bowers.

expenditure of 6,000 or more. They began to starve from the beginning, with incipient scurvy affecting both Oates's old wound and Evans's worsening hand.

On 4 January the other three cheered and waved as Scott, Wilson, Oates, Edgar Evans and Bowers diminished to specks on the horizon, vanishing into whiteness, memory and legend. They then turned on their own desperate journey home. It was to end with Teddy Evans at the brink of death from scurvy at Corner Camp, on the Barrier near Ross Island, in mid-February 1912. He only survived thanks to Lashly and Crean, the former tending him while the latter made a heroic single-handed dash to fetch rescue from Hut Point.

Scott's progress, initially fair, was soon bedevilled by heavy surfaces and *sastrugi* – wind-formed ridges of snow – which made the use of skis so difficult that he temporarily abandoned them. On the 8th they were tent-bound by a minor blizzard (though no worse than had seen Amundsen make 13 miles a day in similar conditions) and on the 9th Scott jubilantly passed Shackleton's furthest south, exactly four years to the day he had been there. It was his last cause for rejoicing. Everyone was now increasingly cold as malnutrition and exhaustion tightened their grip, with only the hope that they would beat Amundsen to the Pole buoying them up. The 'appalling possibility' that they would not came true on 16 January 1912 when Bowers picked out a black spot in the distance. It was a marker

Amundsen and members of his team at the Pole, 15 December 1911.

Oscar Wisting with his dog team on arrival at the South Pole, December 1911.

flag near the remains of a camp, with signs of many dogs.

Amundsen had laid his last depot 95 miles from the Pole on 8-9 December, heading out well-rested on the 10th. As for his outward journey as a whole, his target distance was 15 miles a day (taken overall, his final average was 16 a day). Dogs, sledges and skis all continued to run well through expertise in dealing with the same snow conditions that added to Scott's problems. The weather was generally fine and their main problems were altitude-related, though after they reached a height of 10,500 feet on 12 December, the run south then became a gentle downward slope: Scott's relatively slower ascent up the Beardmore at least gave him more time to acclimatize.

On the 15th at 3pm in the afternoon, with Amundsen skiing in the lead, his drivers cried 'Halt' and told him that the sledgemeters said they were now at the Pole. 'God be thanked' was his simple reaction. All five held the Norwegian flag as they planted it and Amundsen named the area the King Haakon VII Plateau. The formal photographs he took failed, because of damage to his camera, and only Bjaaland's private snaps record the scene. Mindful of the Arctic disputes of Cook and Peary, the Norwegians undertook careful observations over the next two sunny days, and fixed what they thought to be the exact point of the geographical pole about 6 miles further on, marking it with a spare tent and a flag. Here they

The discovery of Amundsen's tent at the Pole by Scott and his men.

left a letter addressed to King Haakon VII of Norway with a request to Scott to forward it, thus verifying their achievement: it was later found with his body. On the 18th they marched out again. Amundsen left behind surplus equipment with a note inviting Scott to take anything he needed and considered including a can of fuel. Unfortunately, believing he would be well supplied, he did not.

Despite seriously missing their bearings for a while near the top of the Axel Heiberg Glacier, the Norwegians and their twelve surviving dogs returned to Framheim on 26 January 1912, fit and well, down their regular depot-line across the Barrier. They had covered over 1,600 miles in 99 days. The type and quality of their dried rations and plenty of fresh meat had prevented any trace of scurvy and the men had even put on weight on the return. *Fram* was already in the offing and on the 30th they sailed for Hobart, Tasmania, where they arrived on 7 March to announce their great news, after a long and stormy passage.

When Scott found Amundsen's flag, and then his tent on 18 January, it was under cloud, wind and a temperature of −30° C. 'Great God!' he wrote in despair, 'this is an awful place and terrible enough for us to have laboured to it without the reward of priority'. Bowers consoled himself with the heroic struggle of the journey and only Oates was sufficiently detached to note that Amundsen 'had his head screwed on right ... they

At the Pole. Left to right: Bowers, Evans, Scott, Oates and Wilson. This is one of several photographs taken by remote control, using a string to work the camera.

seem to have had a comfortable trip with their dog teams very different from our wretched man-hauling'. They left a note at Amundsen's tent, collecting his letter and a spare pair of reindeer mitts for Bowers. A short distance away they then erected a cairn where, wrote Scott, we 'put up our poor slighted Union Jack, and photographed ourselves – mighty cold work all of it'. On the 19th they marched out facing '800 miles of solid dragging – and goodbye to most of the daydreams'.

It was a depressing journey from the beginning. A sail helped to push the sledge on a following wind but this soon became too strong, obscuring their outward tracks and making the small cairns and depots that had marked their course hard to find. Bowers was grateful to retrieve his skis on 31 January, having marched 360 miles without them, but by then Wilson was badly snow-blind and had strained a leg, Oates's toes were turning black and Evans was failing. The largest man of the party, he was suffering most from malnutrition, his cut hand was worsening, his fingernails were dropping off and his extroverted confidence had become withdrawn taciturnity. On 4 February when both he and Scott fell into a crevasse, Scott noted how Evans seemed 'dull and incapable' as they were rescued. On the 8th, after a 'panic' over the loss of a day's supply of biscuit, he ordered a day of relaxed 'geologizing' as they began to descend the Beardmore. This helped morale, though wasting precious time and adding 35lb to their load. (The samples were however to prove important, showing that Antarctica had a warm prehistoric past.)

Things rapidly worsened thereafter, as they lost their way and ran very short of supplies until Wilson spotted their mid-glacier depot. Then on 17 February, after Evans had fallen behind several times, they had to look for

Scott's tent, as it was found, 12 November 1912.

him and found him in a state of mental and physical collapse. He had lost consciousness by the time they got him into the tent and, mercifully, he died in the night. The reasons are unclear but malnutrition, exposure, scurvy and perhaps concussion from one of his falls cover the probabilities. They sat with him for a couple of hours but left no note of what they did with his body, then made a rapid descent to the Barrier.

Here there were plentiful supplies of pony meat at the Shambles Camp but a worrying shortfall of fuel at their Southern Barrier depot. Unlike Amundsen's hermetically sealed containers, Scott's had a leather washer through which the paraffin could leak or evaporate as extreme cold perished the leather, especially if the tin was also exposed to sunshine. Temperatures were now dropping to between −30 and −40° C with the advancing season and they were only making about six or seven miles a day. Oates stopped keeping a diary on the 24th and Wilson on the 27th, leaving Scott the only one recording their slowing progress. On 1 March they arrived at their mid-Barrier depot to find a further critical shortage of fuel, with Oates finally owning up to the desperate state of his frost-bitten feet. By the 6th he could no longer pull and by the 10th probably knew he had no chance. This was the day that Cherry-Garrard, Gerov and the dogs, after confusion over Scott's orders concerning look-out missions and the rescue of Evans and Lashly, finally abandoned a six-day wait for the Polar party at One Ton depot and headed for home. On the 11th Scott was

around 55 miles from One Ton, with seven days food, little fuel, and the probability that both would run out two days march before the depot.

The bitter wind, low temperatures and failing strength now kept them all longer in the tent, and they began to lose track of dates. Scott had ordered Wilson to share out all their opiates, sufficient for painless suicide: they were not used. On what was probably the evening of the 16th, Oates's gangrenous feet made it impossible for him to continue and he went to sleep hoping not to wake. When he did there was a blizzard blowing and it was his thirty-second birthday. No-one stopped him when, as Scott recorded, he said 'I am just going outside and may be some time', opened the tent and was gone.

On 21 March the last three were 11 miles from One Ton, already trapped for two days in their tent by another blizzard, and at the end of their fuel and rations. Scott was now in the worst condition with a gangrenous right foot and had started writing his last letters as early as the 16th. Wilson and Bowers, who was still the fittest, considered a joint dash to the depot for fuel and supplies but the weather prevented any move. Beyond One Ton (if they could find it) there were 130 miles to go and Scott may have argued it was better that their bodies and records be found together than lost separately in forlorn hopes. Tragically, of course, had the depot been laid where originally intended they would already have reached it. Exactly when and how they died is unknown but the last entry in Scott's diary is 29 March. Even at the end, his literary gift did not desert him:

Had we lived, I should have had a tale to tell of the hardihood, endurance and courage of my companions which would have stirred the heart of every Englishman. These rough notes and our dead bodies must tell the tale ...

Outside ... it remains a scene of whirling drift. I do not think we can hope for any better things now. We shall stick it out to the end, but we are getting weaker, of course, and the end cannot be far.
It seems a pity, but I do not think I can write more.
  R. Scott.

For God's sake look after our people.

The bodies were discovered seven months later. Atkinson and twelve others had been resupplied by *Terra Nova* and were left with the dilemma of whether to search for the dead or to try and rescue Campbell's party, which had spent a second winter unrelieved, living in a snow cave on the coast of Victoria Land. It proved a short search for Scott, the tent being found two weeks march south from Cape Evans on 12 November 1912. Atkinson recovered their papers, the sledge and geological samples, and various personal and small items, before collapsing the tent on the bodies and building a large cairn over the spot. A search for Oates proved fruitless, only his abandoned sleeping bag being found. On the 27th, Campbell and his men miraculously turned up on their own at Hut Point. It was above here, on Observation Hill, that a large wooden cross was erected as a monument to Scott and his four companions as soon as *Terra Nova* arrived in January 1913, now with a recovered Teddy Evans back in command. It still stands, bearing their names and a line chosen by Cherry-Garrard from Tennyson's *Ulysses*: 'To strive, to seek, to find and not to yield.'

The start of the search party from Cape Evans, *Terra Nova* expedition; a photograph taken by Frank Debenham.

The final entry in Scott's diary, 29 March 1912.

Food for the Race to the Pole

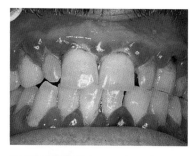

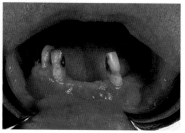

Swollen and inflamed gums in scurvy.

Clinical photograph of a mouth showing the extreme effects of scurvy.

The role of vitamins in preventing many diseases had not yet been shown in 1911, the year of Scott and Amundsen's attempts to reach the South Pole and just a year before the Polish scientist Casimir Funk gave vitamins their name. For the avoidance of scurvy, the disease caused by a lack of vitamin C in the diet, explorers could only have faith in the well-known recommendations of the eighteenth-century Royal Naval surgeon Dr James Lind*, on the one hand, while remembering, on the other, the near-opposite belief that canned meats, when subject to spoilage, could contain a poisonous agent that caused scurvy. Little was known about deficiencies in B vitamins and explorers had to rely on common sense, and the previous experiences and reports of other expeditions. Scott's arrangements in 1911 had therefore progressed little from those made for his previous *Discovery* expedition in 1901. He had at that time summarized his belief in the causes of scurvy as follows:

> For centuries, and until quite recently, it was believed that the antidote to scurvy lay in vegetable acids; scurvy grass was sought by the older voyages, and finally lime-juice was made, and remains, a legal necessity for ships travelling on the high seas. Behind this belief lies a vast amount of evidence, but a full consideration of this evidence is beset with immense difficulties. For instance, although it is an undoubted fact that with the introduction of lime-juice scurvy was largely diminished, yet is apt to be forgotten that there were other causes which might have contributed to this result; for at the same time sea voyages were being largely reduced by steam power, and owners were forced to provide much better food for their men...
>
> I understand that scurvy is now believed to be ptomaine poisoning, caused by the virus of the bacterium of decay in meat, and in plain language, as long as a man continues to assimilate this poison he is bound to get worse, and when he ceases to add to the quantity taken the system tends to throw it off, and the patient recovers.
>
> It has been pointed out that scurvy depends largely on environment, and there can be no doubt that severe or insanitary conditions of life contribute to the ravages of the disease. Indeed, we saw how this might be from the outbreak in our western party, but I do not think such conditions can be regarded as prime cause.
>
> R.F. Scott, *The Voyage of the Discovery*

According to Scott's listings, his daily rations for the *Discovery* expedition contained 8.6 oz of protein, 4.4 oz of fat and 15.6 oz of carbohydrate. This works out to be about 3,500 calories per day. The amount of food (in ounces) carried per day, per man, as originally outlined by Scott was: biscuit, 12.0; oatmeal, 1.5; pemmican (preserved meat), 7.6; red ration, 1.1; plasmon (meat concentrate), 2.0; pea flour, 1.5; cheese, 2.0; chocolate, 1.1; cocoa, 0.7; sugar, 3.8. In addition, small quantities of tea, onion

*In 1753, Lind first demonstrated the efficacy of lemon juice as an anti-scorbutic, although the less effective lime-juice became more widely used at sea in the nineteenth century.

powder, pepper and salt were available. Scott deserves much credit for his attention to the rations on this expedition. He carefully compared his daily allowance of 35.5 oz to those of earlier polar explorers, including McClintock (42 oz), Nares (40 oz) and Parry (20 oz), noting that Parry's sledging trips were short and that his party must still have been famished.

On 18 August 1911, while Scott's team continued to make preparations at Cape Evans, Dr Edward Atkinson, its naval surgeon, gave a lecture to the men that summarized what Scott believed at that time:

> Atkinson lectured on 'Scurvy' last night. He spoke clearly and slowly, but the disease is anything but precise. He gave a little summary of its history afloat and the remedies long in use in the Navy.
>
> He described the symptoms with some detail. Mental depression, debility, syncope, petechia, livid patches, spongy gums, lesions, swellings, and so on to

Wilson, Cherry-Garrard and Ford examine a Leopard seal.

Seal being butchered by members of Amundsen's crew on the *Fram* expedition.

things that are worse. He passed to some of the theories held and remedies tried in accordance with them. Sir Almroth Wright has hit the truth, he thinks, in finding increased acidity of blood – acid intoxication – by methods only possible in recent years ... so far for diagnosis, but it does not bring us much closer to the cause, preventives, or remedies. Practically we are much as we were before, but the lecturer proceeded to deal with the practical side.

In brief, he holds the first cause to be tainted food, but secondary or contributory causes may be even more potent in developing the disease, damp, cold, overexertion, bad air, bad light, in fact any condition exceptional to normal healthy existence. Remedies are merely to change these conditions for the better. Dietetically, fresh vegetables are the best curatives – the lecturer was doubtful of fresh meat, but admitted its possibility in Polar climate; lime juice only useful if regularly taken. He discussed lightly the relative values of vegetable stuffs, doubtful of those containing abundance of phosphates such as lentils ...

His remarks were extremely sound and practical as usual. He proved the value of fresh meat in Polar regions.

Packing sugar for sledging rations, January 1912, *Terra Nova* expedition.

Scurvy seems very far away from us this time; yet after our *Discovery* experience, one feels that no trouble can be too great or no precaution too small to be adopted to keep it at bay. Therefore such an evening as last was well spent. It is certain we shall not have the disease here, but one cannot foresee equally certain avoidance in the southern journey to come. All one can do is to take every possible precaution.

L. Huxley, *Scott's Last Expedition*, vol. 2, 1913 edition.

On 24 October 1911 two motor sledges started ahead of Scott's main group, hauling material, but they quickly broke down and had to be abandoned. Scott himself left on 1 November with eight ponies, each with a sled. Dogs were used, following later, but were not to be taken to the Pole. Travel was difficult; the ponies sank in the snow but, even more important, they suffered terribly as they stood at night when sweat turned to ice on their bodies. Though dogs did not suffer from the harsh conditions, Scott did not appreciate their advantage over ponies. He disowned the idea that dogs could eat dogs and especially that men could eat dogs. Before his final support party left, Scott made the fateful decision to increase his group going to the Pole from four to five men, even though the food had been apportioned and tenting provided for only four. At this point they were all man-hauling, which undoubtedly placed their bodies under greater stress and would have had an impact on vitamin levels. Perhaps Scott should have followed the 1890 recommendation of the US Arctic explorer Robert E. Peary that 'every increase in the party, beyond the number absolutely essential [adds to] an element of danger and failure'.

Yet for a brief time all seemed well. Just three days later Christmas was celebrated with such a plentiful supper that Scott wrote they had eaten too much:

> I must write a word of our supper last night. We had four courses. The first, pemmican, full whack, with slices of horse meat flavoured with onion and curry powder and thickened with biscuits; then an arrowroot, cocoa and biscuit hoosh [thick soup or stew] sweetened; then a plum-pudding; then cocoa with raisins, and finally desert [sic] of caramels and ginger. After the feast it was difficult to move. Wilson and I couldn't finish our plates of plum-pudding. We have all slept splendidly and feel thoroughly warm – such is the effect of full feeding.

L. Huxley, *Scott's Last Expedition*, vol. 2

However, the group arrived at the Pole physically exhausted, with their morale further undermined by discovering that Amundsen had been there before them. The fateful return journey started on 25 January. Soon they were frequently stalled by very bad weather, exhausted and barely making each depot before running out of food, even when on partial rations. By 14 February, Scott was writing:

> There is no getting away from the fact that we are not pulling strongly. Probably none of us: Wilson's leg still troubles him and he doesn't like to trust himself on ski; but the worst case is Evans, who is giving us serious anxiety. This morning he suddenly disclosed a huge blister on his foot. It delayed us on the march, when he had to have his crampon readjusted. Sometimes I fear he is going from bad to worse, but I trust he will pick up again when we come to steady work on ski like this afternoon. He is hungry and so is Wilson. We can't risk opening our food again, and as cook at present I am serving something under full allowance. We are inclined to get slack and slow with our camping arrangements, and small delays increase. I have talked of the matter tonight and hope for improvement. We cannot do distance without the hours. The next depot some thirty miles away and nearly 3 days food in hand.

L. Huxley, *Scott's Last Expedition*, vol. 2

Then came two terrible fatalities. The first was the death of Petty Officer Evans, a large man, who complained that he received the same ration as the rest of them but that his body required more. In retrospect, one can say that his claim was well founded, although Scott formally noted his belief that concussion from one of several falls may have contributed to his physical and mental collapse. By 5 March they still had a long way to go, but with a favourable wind still made nine miles that day. Yet Scott knew things were bad:

> Lunch – Regret to say going from bad to worse. We got a slant of wind yesterday afternoon, and going on five hours we converted our wretched morning run of three and a half miles to something over nine. We went to bed on a cup of cocoa and pemmican solid with the chill off. The result is telling on all, but mainly Oates, whose feet are in a wretched condition. One swelled up tremendously last night and he is very lame this morning. We started march on tea and pemmican as last night – we pretend to prefer the pemmican this way.

> L. Huxley, *Scott's Last Expedition*, vol. 1

Oates indeed had started failing rapidly, particularly with very bad feet but by the time he walked out of the tent to his death on 17 March all three of the others were also suffering in various ways, particularly Dr Wilson. On Wednesday, 21 March they were stopped by a sub-zero blizzard and never left their tent again.

The last entry in Scott's journal has already been quoted (see page 79) but he also left a message to the public including his explanation of the causes of his party's death:

> 1) The loss of the pony transport in March 1911 obliged me to start later than I had intended and obliged the limits of the stuff transported to be narrowed.
> 2) The weather throughout the outward journey and especially the long gale in 83° south stopped us.
> 3) The soft snow and lower reaches of glacier again reduced the pace.

> L.Huxley, *Scott's Last Expedition*, vol. 1

He also added that he thought they had brought enough food and that the depots were properly placed.

There have been many analyses of the Scott expedition and the reasons why his polar party did not survive their return. The weakest link in the end was the food and nutrition. This failure was not entirely Scott's fault, because the state of knowledge at that time was insufficient to formulate the diet properly. None the less it is clear that malnutrition occurred and, especially with Evans, scurvy is also suspected.

In his dramatic account of the *Terra Nova* expedition, *The Worst Journey in the World*, Apsley Cherry-Garrard stated: 'I have always had a doubt whether the weather conditions were sufficient to cause the tragedy'. He went on to indicate that even in 1922 when he wrote his book, it could be shown that Scott's party had insufficient calories:

> Of course the whole business simply bristles with 'ifs': if Scott had taken the dogs and succeeded in getting them up the Beardmore: if we had not lost those ponies on the depot journey: if the dogs had not been taken so far and the One Ton

Depot had been laid: if a pony and an extra oil had been depoted on the barrier: if a four-man party had been taken to the Pole: if I had disobeyed my instructions and gone for One Ton, killing dogs as necessary: or even if I had just gone on a few miles and left some food and fuel under a flag upon a cairn: if they had been first at the Pole: if it had been any other season but that...

Cherry-Garrard, *The Worst Journey in the World*

Cherry-Garrard was deeply affected by the failed rescue attempt that he and dog-handler Dimitri Gerov made with dogs to One Ton Depot at the time Scott was still travelling. Scott had left orders that the dogs were

Clissold the cook making bread at Cape Evans, 25 March 1911. *Terra Nova* expedition.

not to be pushed hard and, in addition, dog food had not been left at One Ton Depot because of transportation and weather problems. After waiting a few days, Cherry-Garrard and Gerov had returned to Hut Point. Many think Cherry-Garrard spent the rest of his life believing that he could have saved Scott if he had gone further than One Ton, killing dogs as needed, but this would have been against Scott's original order.

Not only did Scott's Pole party meet their end in tragic nutritional conditions but his last support party, during their return, likewise encountered scurvy and other serious food problems. A look at Scott's rations would not reveal anything to appeal to us today, nor does it tell us its nutritional value; however, an analysis of Scott's diet in comparison with other expeditions is shown on page 86. Although these figures are estimates because no contemporary analyses were or could have been made, they indicate deplorable nutrition. Much of this was unavoidable because of the ignorance about vitamins at that time but the calorie deficiency need not have occurred. It is also likely that deteriorative chemical interactions could have greatly reduced the diet's nutritional value. For example, data on the composition of Scott's biscuits that shows they contained sodium bicarbonate. This is not surprising in itself but it could

Sledging rations (per day)

Amundsen
From 1910-12
(dog-driving)

Scott
Discovery 1901-04
(man-hauling)

Scott
Terra Nova 1910-13
(man-hauling: Polar Plateau)

Team Polar 2000
Royal Marines - North Pole
(man-hauling: 250lb sledges)

Breakfast

Amundsen	Scott (Discovery)	Wt (g)	kCal	Scott (Terra Nova)	Wt (g)	kCal	Team Polar 2000	Wt (g)	kCal
–	Cocoa	20	±45	Cocoa	±30	73	Chocolate drink (dry wt)	60	228
Oatmeal	Oatmeal	40	163	(Tea/Coffee)			Hot cereal (dry wt)	90	370
(in biscuits and				–			Apple flakes	±50	320
pemmican)				–			Energy drinks x1.5	c300	194

Supplements

Amundsen	Scott (Discovery)	Wt (g)	kCal	Scott (Terra Nova)	Wt (g)	kCal	Team Polar 2000	Wt (g)	kCal
Biscuits[1]	Biscuits	340	c1300	Biscuits[2] x8	c450	1728	Biscuits x6	55	332
Chocolate	Chocolate	31	±160	(Chocolate)			Chocolate raisins	±100	400
Sugar (in biscuits)	Sugar	108	430	Sugar	85	336	Energy bar	±50	163
–	Cheese	57	±450	Butter & cheese	65	452	Protein drink	c±50	189
Milk powder				(Milk)			Energy drink	200	194

Main Meals

Amundsen	Scott (Discovery)	Wt (g)	kCal	Scott (Terra Nova)	Wt (g)	kCal	Team Polar 2000	Wt (g)	kCal
Pemmican and	Pemmican	215	c1000	Bovril Pemmican	430	2004	Pasta carb x2	±350	700
(vegetables	Plasmon	57	c150	(curry powder[3])			Chicken noodles x2	±350	700
in pemmican)	(meat concentrate)			(Essence of beef rations -			Chicken balti x2	±350	700
–	Pea Flour	43	±130	Brand & Co)			Beef and potato	±350	700
				(Rice – 1 large bag found			[NB if these made up from dry, divide		
				and two smaller, empty)			by 3: total for this section then ±450g]		

Puddings

Amundsen	Scott (Discovery)	Wt (g)	kCal	Scott (Terra Nova)	Team Polar 2000	Wt (g)	kCal
biscuits	Other:			–	Choc chip pud x2	c±150	459
containing oatmeal,	Red ration	31	?		Apple custard	c100	350
sugar & dried milk	Described by Scott as				Apple and rice	c100	304
	a nondescript compound				Peach & pineapple	c200	320
Pemmican	of bacon and pea-flour.						
specially prepared:	(Tea, onion powder,						
with added vegtables	pepper, salt)						
and later oatmeal							

TOTALS:

Amundsen	Scott (Discovery)	Wt (g)	kCal	Scott (Terra Nova)	Wt (g)	kCal	Team Polar 2000	Wt (g)	kCal
			±3750			4593	(>2.5-3 x UK male intake)		6600

'Our provisions consisted of only these 4 kinds, and the combination turned out right enough. We did not suffer from a craving either for fat or sugar, though the want of these substances is very commonly felt on such journeys as ours.' (Amundsen)

Statistical weight and calorie information unavailable for *Fram* expedition.

(Calories required to meet physical exertion: 6000 kCal – a shortfall of over 1000 kCal per day per man – leading to starvation, exhaustion and eventual scurvy)

Weights & nutritional breakdown

	Wt (g)	%		Wt (g)	%		Wt (g)	%
Protein	244g	24%	Protein	257g	24%	Protein	280g	10%
Fat	124g	12%	Fat	210g	19%	Fat	260g	9%
Carbohydrate	442g	44%	Carbohydrate	417g	39%	Carbohydrate	870g	31%
Other	190g	19%	Other	±200g	19%	Other	1390g	50%
Total weight	±1000g		**Total weight**	±1080g		**Total weight**	±2800g	

NB For Team Polar 2000, the overall weight depends largely on the extent to which the meals are made up from powdered/dried ingredients.

Photograph taken to demonstrate the use of Heinz beans as a staple on the *Terra Nova* expedition at base camp.

Sledging ration, one man, per day. *Terra Nova* expedition.

Additional information/notes

Amundsen
From 1910-12
(dog-driving)

Lunch:
[1] 3-4 dry oatmeal biscuits, that was all. If one wanted a drink, one could mix snow with the biscuit.'
(Amundsen)

Scott
Discovery 1901-04
(man-hauling)

*Scott 'carefully compared his daily allowance of 35.5oz with those of earlier polar explorers including McClintock (42oz), Nares (40oz) and Parry (20oz), noting that Parry's sledging trips were short and that his party must have been famished.'

Summer sledging supper:
'supper... consisted of a hoosh [stew] made of pemmican, cheese, oatmeal, pea-flour and bacon.'

Scott
Terra Nova 1910-13
(man-hauling: Polar Plateau)

[2] NB Scott's biscuits contained sodium bicarb. which lowered their vitamin content.

[3] Curry powder was used to disguise the flavour of meat.

Food was half-cooked towards the end. A primus stove was used for cooking, and the fuel was running out.

'We are running short of provisions... as cook at present I am serving something under full allowance.'
Scott, returning from Pole,
14 Feb 1912.

Team Polar 2000
Royal Marines - North Pole
(man-hauling: 250lb sledges)

Team Polar 2000 refers to the Royal Marines' recent expedition to reach the North Pole.

All weights, measures and calorie values are given as approximations and for comparative purposes only.

Sources:
Polar Journeys: The Role of Food and Nutrition in Early Exploration, Robert E. Feeney, 1998.
Royal Marines 'Team Polar 2000' website: www.teampolar2000.co.uk
Antarctic philately website: www.south-pole.com

Also used:
www.cyberdiet.com (calorie counts)
www.diy.co.uk (units conversion)

A Knorr powdered soup packet, taken on the *Fram* expedition.

have lowered some of the vitamin content on baking, possibly destroying all of the thiamine. Because the biscuits were an important source of thiamine, its loss could have been critical, leading to incipient beri-beri, which causes inflammation of the nervous system and paralysis, especially of outer limbs.

Amundsen's Norwegian expedition was profoundly different in planning, execution and outcome. He had analysed Shackleton's *Nimrod* expedition and concluded that larger depots were needed along the route. Amundsen's idea that fresh, undercooked meat prevented scurvy was a critical point. However, for energy on the long stages he still needed pemmican. A perhaps fortunate set-back occurred when the food manu-facturer, Armour of Chicago, who believed that Amundsen planned to head for the North Pole and had already supported Peary's successful expedition there in 1908–09, cancelled their promise to give free pemmican. From Amundsen's polar work he knew that richer, sugar-based foods might cause problems for some men, including stomach ailments, constipation and diarrhoea, all of which could create great difficulties on a polar trail. So he had pemmican specially prepared, first adding vegetables and later oatmeal for fibre.

After setting up Framheim, the Norwegian base camp, on 27 January 1911 at the Bay of Whales, 200 seals and the same number of penguins were killed and frozen for food. Served twice daily for lunch and supper, fresh or deep-frozen seal was the main dish at the base. The men also received cloudberry preserves which were a rich source of vitamins. Amundsen directed that the seal meat must be undercooked, thereby saving much of the vitamin C. All through the subsequent winter Amundsen's group stored up vitamin C, vitamin D and, probably most important of all, the vitamin B complex in their bodies. They ate whole-meal bread fortified with wheat germ and leavened with fresh yeast (both later known as good sources of B vitamins). When the party laid their depots southwards, they also did so at good march intervals with plenty of food in each place. The last pre-laid main depot being 420 miles from the Pole at 82° south.

Amundsen also recognized the value of the traditional Norwegian diet, which formed the basis for sledging provisions:

> I have never considered it necessary to take a whole grocery shop with me when sledging; the food should be simple and nourishing and that is enough – a rich and varied menu is for people who have no work to do. Besides pemmican we had biscuits, milk powder and chocolate... Milk powder is a comparatively new commodity with us but it deserves to be better known. It came from the district of Jaederen. Neither heat nor cold, dryness or wet could hurt it; we had large quantities of it lying out in small thin linen bags in every possible state of the weather...We are bringing all the purveyors of our sledging samples of their goods that have made the journey to the South Pole and back in gratitude for the kind assistance they afforded us.

Amundsen, *The South Pole*, vol. 1

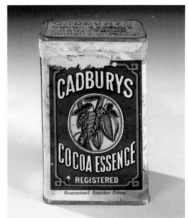

Johansen packing the tubes of dried milk used by Amundsen as a dietary supplement on the *Fram* expedition.

Cadbury's supplied cocoa for both the British and Norwegian expeditions. This tin was carried by Amundsen on the *Fram* expedition.

Amundsen had provisioned so prudently that he actually had spare foodstuffs to bring back to the temperate zone as souvenirs.

The Norwegians left Framheim for the Pole on 20 October with an even greater margin of safety in their depot supplies because of the very late reduction of the planned party from eight to five. When he reached his last depot at 82° south, Amundsen was carrying supplies for 100 days, until 6 February, but was hoping to return to Framheim by 31 January. Even this estimate did not include the depot already at 82°, plus others further north, so even if he missed all these on the return, his supplies were still adequate to make it back with a week to spare. Furthermore, the party also slaughtered surplus dogs *en route* to feed the others, as well as themselves, and placed some of the carcasses and small supplies at further small depots for their return. On the journey south the Norwegian men even savoured the idea of eating the dogs:

> the thought of the fresh dog cutlets that awaited us when we got to the top [of the Axel Heiberg Glacier] made our mouths water. In the course of time we had so habituated ourselves to the idea of the approaching slaughter of dogs that this event did not appear to us as horrible as it would otherwise have done.

Amundsen, *The South Pole*, vol. 2

On re-stocking their provisions they also made up their supplies in such a form that they could count them instead of weighing them out:

> Our pemmican was in rations of one-half kilogram (1 pound 1½ ounces). The chocolate was divided into small pieces, as chocolate always is, so that we knew

what each piece weighed. Our milk powder was put up in bags of 10½ ounces – just enough for a meal. Our biscuits possessed the same property – they could be counted, but this was a tedious business, as they were rather small. On this occasion we had to count 6,000 biscuits. Our provisions consisted of only these four kinds, and the combinations turned out right enough. We did not suffer from a craving either for fat or sugar, though the want of these substances is very commonly felt on such journeys as ours. In our biscuits we had an excellent product, consisting of oatmeal, sugar and dried milk. Sweetmeats, jam, fruit, cheese, etc., we had left behind at Framheim.

Amundsen, *The South Pole*, vol.2

At 82° south, on their return, they had pemmican and seal steaks, with chocolate pudding for dessert. Three dogs had died and they had to kill one, reducing them to thirteen. When the dead ones were fed to the living, they seemed to liven up. The dogs were put on double rations of pemmican, seal meat, biscuits and even chocolate later on. On reaching the big depot at 80° the party considered they were home and left it 'still large, well supplied, and well marked, so it is not impossible that it may be found useful later.' On 25 January they returned to Framheim with a dozen dogs, as originally planned, and with men and dogs all in good shape.

Both noted and hidden in the many versions and stories of these two expeditions are the dietary reasons for their successes and failures. Racing from depot to depot and killing his dogs, Amundsen did not once appear to be short of nutritious food. It is well known that Scott, Wilson and Bowers were almost out of food when they died, only a single bag of rice and one or two biscuits being reclaimed from their tent. Explanations of the disaster that overcame Scott's party have tended to dwell on the terrible weather he encountered and the vital time expended on scientific observation and specimen collection. This has rather overlooked the major difference between Scott and Amundsen in the matter of food – both in its quantity and quality – and especially so given Scott's reliance on man-hauling rather than on dogs. Underlying this, as we now know, is the critical fact that food is metabolized and energy generated by the catalytic fires of vitamins and some trace-metal ions whose retention varies depending on levels of both prior and ongoing intake, as well as on energy consumption. The application of this knowledge and that of other discoveries relating to calorie intake and nutrition during polar journeys, were used in ration planning and development for the two World Wars of the twentieth century and have also contributed to the development of nutrition programmes for space and modern polar expeditions.

A can of powdered meat taken on the *Fram* expedition.

The Great White Silence
Antarctic Exploration and Film

Men dressed in explorers' furs advertising one of the lantern-lectures by Sir Ernest Shackleton, December 1909.

In his account of the list of equipment taken on board the *Nimrod* as it set sail for Antarctica in 1907, Ernest Shackleton concludes with a novel addition and explains its possible uses:

> We took also with us a cinematograph machine in order that we might place on record the curious movements and habits of the seals and penguins, and give the people at home a graphic idea of what it means to haul sledges over the ice and snow.

This is a strikingly cautious assessment of the value of a motion picture record, and it indicates in a number of ways the particular apprehension over the role of the cinematograph that came to characterize its use in the 'heroic' era of polar exploration. In sharp contrast, just a few years later, the words of King George V spoken after seeing Herbert Ponting's film of the Scott expedition reveal an overwhelming belief in the power of motion pictures: 'I wish that every British boy could see this film. The story should be known to all the youth of the Nation, for it will help to foster the spirit of adventure on which the Empire was founded.' The two visions of the Antarctic exploration film given here – one the suggestion of possible light entertainment, the other professing a belief that such a film expressed a special adventurous and noble spirit – were central to the production and exhibition of Antarctic exploration films during the comparatively short period of their existence.

Ponting at work in his Cape Evans darkroom on the *Terra Nova* expedition, 24 March 1911.

The classical era of polar exploration and the start of motion pictures took place at almost exactly the same time. Motion-picture films, projected on a screen, became known to the public in 1896, and they rapidly spread the world over. Film was developing primarily as an entertainment medium but its value as a tool for scientific discovery was appreciated in some corners in the 1890s. Dr Doyen, a French surgeon, filmed his operations; German botanist Wilhelm Pfeffer used time-lapse photography to record plant growth; Cambridge ethnologist A.C. Haddon took a cine camera on his pioneering trip to the Torres Straits; and it was reported that Carsten Borchgrevink's expedition to Antarctica was going to take a Newman and Guardia 35mm camera, ushering in the age of the polar film.

There is no evidence, however, that Louis Bernacchi, the expedition's photographer, used the cine camera, nor is there any record of such films being exhibited. All that exists on film today is a single shot of the expedition's financier, publisher Sir George Newnes, bidding them farewell – a record made by a commercial film company. Film was in its infancy as a medium of record. Film technology was still being developed and standardized, although the Newman camera selected by Borchgrevink was already noted for its dependability and a later model would be the

Ponting filming 'watering the ship',
14 December 1910, *Terra Nova* expedition.

choice of Herbert Ponting. Most films in the 1890s were no more than a
minute in length, thought of as 'animated photographs' rather than as
something with duration or great documentary value. A film record
therefore played no part in Scott's 1901 *Discovery* expedition but by the
time Shackleton set sail for Antarctica in August 1907, the film industry,
and more importantly film exhibition, had moved on considerably.

The film of Shackleton's 1907–09 expedition, when he came to within
97 miles of the pole and returned home a national hero, does not survive.
Although this film only covered activity at the base camp and did not
follow Shackleton and his team on their journey south, it was nevertheless
a substantial record. Dr Eric Marshall, the expedition's surgeon,
cartographer and novice cine cameraman, shot over 4,000 feet of film
(approximately 70 minutes), which was shown extensively over Britain on
Shackleton's return, sometimes accompanying his own lectures and
sometimes exhibited in its own right as *Nearest the South Pole*. Films in
1909 could now be much longer but, crucially, there were more places, and
places of a suitable nature, in which to show them. There were no cinemas
in the 1890s, when films were first shown: they were instead then
exhibited as part of theatre variety programmes, in photographic salons or
on fairgrounds. As the medium developed and became progressively

popular, special auditoria designed solely for films began to be built, and 1909 was at the start of a great boom in the construction of cinemas in Britain. Shackleton's films were a success primarily because of his popularity but also because there existed the means of exhibiting them to a wide audience.

Films of travel and exploration were becoming popular, as audiences came to see the world around them brought to the local cinema and were told of the thrilling exploits involved in bringing such pictures to the screen. The Shackleton film therefore appears to have been a commercial success (something that would soon grow to become a major consideration in Antarctic expeditions to come) but its value as a record was probably minimal. The public may have discovered the 'curious movements and habits of seals and penguins' and may have been a little wiser about what it took to haul a sledge, but Marshall's film probably had little further real documentary value. However, there would now come onto the scene two photographers whose skills and vision matched the grand expeditions on which they found themselves: Herbert Ponting and Frank Hurley.

Herbert Ponting was a masterly photographer. His work in Japan in the 1900s alone would have won him a worthy note in photographic history, had he not joined Scott's 1910–12 expedition, where he was to produce some of the most enduring images of polar exploration. What is remarkable is that his skills should likewise, so readily have transferred to the cine camera. Ponting had never used a cine camera before but film historian Kevin Brownlow has given him the highest accolade by declaring that 'Herbert Ponting was to the expedition film what Charles Rosher [Mary Pickford's cameraman] was to the feature picture – a photographer and cinematographer of unparalleled artistry'. Ponting's skill in picture composition was evident from his earlier photographic work, but he also brought a dramatic sense to the filming from his experience as a lecturer. Throughout his work on the Scott expedition, Ponting imagined how he would present such scenes to an audience back home and selected, composed and arranged his material accordingly. Scott himself humorously coined the verb 'ponting' and 'to pont' to describe being 'directed' for the benefit of the camera. Ponting had also thought ahead when it came to his film's commercial value. An agreement was drawn up assigning 40 per cent of the profits to the expedition, 40 per cent to the company producing and distributing the film (Gaumont), and 20 per cent to Ponting.

The release structure of Ponting's films was determined by the nature of the expedition and a need to keep up audience interest over the two years that it would take. Ponting joined the *Terra Nova* in New Zealand in November 1910 with both a Prestwich and a Newman Sinclair cine camera whose manufacturer, Arthur S. Newman, had given him intensive instruction in its use and had added special ebonite fittings to prevent

Ponting and his cine camera, *Terra Nova* expedition.

Ponting filming skua gulls on the *Terra Nova* expedition, 7 January 1911.

Ponting's fingers from freezing to the camera. He also took an initial 15,000 feet of negative film of which he had shot and developed on site 8,000 feet before the *Terra Nova* returned to New Zealand from the Antarctic in January 1911. This film was delivered to Britain and edited by Gaumont into a 2,000-foot release (lasting around 30 minutes) entitled *With Captain Scott, R.N. to the South Pole*. This was first shown in November 1911. Ponting's second batch of film was released by Gaumont as the 'second series' of *With Captain Scott, R.N. to the South Pole*, in two 1,500-foot parts, which were first shown in September and October 1912, respectively, and featured the final scenes of the polar party, including sequences where they demonstrated sledge-hauling and life inside their tent. By this time, of course, Scott and his final polar party were all dead, and news of Amundsen's success in winning the race to the pole dented the film's commercial appeal.

The bodies were discovered in November 1912. Ponting then began to devote his life to the promotion of the Scott legend and to recouping the investment he made in 1914 when he purchased all rights in the film from Gaumont for £5,000. This he did against a waning audience interest and much of the bitterness of his later years was due to the public's insufficient awe at a story which he progressively built up and romanticized, as the

Scott tragedy evolved into myth. The film came to be released in a bewildering variety of forms. In its original release form it had been three short films of around 30 minutes duration each. The films were re-edited and released in America in 1913, after Scott's death had been reported, as *The Undying Story of Captain Scott*. Ponting then constantly lectured with the films, giving a Royal Command performance in May 1914 (where he elicited the comments by King George V quoted above), and then throughout World War I, emphasizing the call to patriotic sacrifice but now to dwindling audiences. In 1924 Ponting re-edited the films once more as a feature-length documentary, *The Great White Silence*, which followed on from the 1921 publication of his book *The Great White South*. This film, which exists today (while the original 1911–12 releases do not), was 7,300 feet long – that is, around two hours in length – and was released by the New Era company. Reviews were complimentary, marvelling at the hardships endured and praising both the film's patriotic virtues and 'extremely clever studies of Antarctic life', while pointing out that the final scenes were, of necessity, heavily dependent on still pictures, diagrams and subtitles. Scott's adventures were already of another age and the film was not a notable success.

Ponting failed in his subsequent attempts to sell his films to the nation, an appropriate film archiving body not existing at that time, and in 1933 he produced a sound version of his films, now entitled *90° South*, released by New Era once again and lasting 75 minutes. Ponting himself provided the film's commentary and years of lecturing to its images tell in his polished and succinct words. This time the reviews were more enthusiastic, as reviewers newly aware of the documentary as an art form rightly praised Ponting's artistry. But Ponting's problem, and that of any of the polar exploration films, was in attracting a mass cinema audience that was primarily interested in the escapism of the fiction genre. Appeals to patriotism have never been enough when it comes to selling a film to the public. Ponting was a great film maker but he invested too much faith (and too much money) in his Antarctic footage, and remained with it too long. However, his film survives in its 1924 (silent) and 1933 (sound) versions, and with the passing of time grows in stature as one of the certain masterpieces of documentary in the earliest years of cinema.

The other great figure in Antarctic cinematography is Frank Hurley. Hurley was an Australian who had begun to build up a local reputation for himself as a picture-postcard photographer of initiative and style, when he persuaded Douglas Mawson, veteran of Shackleton's 1907–09 expedition, to take him as the photographer and cinematographer on Mawson's own first Antarctic venture in 1911. This expedition landed at Commonwealth Bay in January 1912 and eventually divided into two parties, with Hurley joining Bob Bage and Eric Webb to secure an accurate relocation for the South Magnetic Pole, while Mawson went eastwards with the ill-fated 'Cherub' Ninnis and Xavier Mertz. Hurley discovered all the virtues of

'Ponko' the Penguin; one of the earliest examples of film merchandise created. The label of this stuffed toy reads:

' "Ponko" The Penguin is designed from my photographic studies of penguins taken during Capt. Scott's South Pole expedition and described by me at the Philharmonic Hall, London, Herbert G. Ponting'.

Antarctic filming – the tonal values of the icebound landscape, the sharp southern light and the exotic animal life – and its many disadvantages – the agonies of threading the film or operating a hand-turned camera with frost-bitten fingers, the need to melt huge blocks of ice in the developing

Hurley filming from his sledge, *Endurance* expedition.

process and the constant need to keep the equipment clean and in working order.

In total, Hurley recorded the departure from Hobart in the *Aurora*, the journey south, wildlife at Macquarie Island and Cape Denison, the 600-mile trek to locate the South Magnetic Pole and the desperate return, with both Bage and Hurley afflicted by snow-blindness. Hurley had recorded Mawson, Ninnis and Mertz in their tent prior to their departure, but later had to leave in the *Aurora* before he knew of the fate of Mawson's party. Lieutenant Belgrave Ninnis died falling into a crevasse; Dr Mertz probably from vitamin A poisoning caused by eating dog livers. Only Mawson survived but was forced to spend another winter in the Antarctic ice, while the *Aurora* (compelled by conditions to return home rather than rescue the others at that time) returned to Australia. The expedition's finances did not allow for a second relief voyage, and Hurley's film, swiftly released by West's Pictures in July 1913 as *Life in the Antarctic*, both proved greatly popular and helped raise much of the money needed to fund the rescue of Mawson and his men later in the year. The finished film, which Hurley later retitled *Home of the Blizzard* after Mawson's book of the expedition, was some 4,500 feet long (75 minutes). It was also screened in Britain, thereby ensuring Hurley's presence on the next Antarctic expedition, that of Sir Ernest Shackleton.

Hurley's participation in Shackleton's Imperial Trans-Antarctic

Expedition of 1914-16 in fact enabled it to go ahead. Shackleton was only able to complete the financing of his expedition when he secured a deal with a Fleet Street syndicate which put forward the money in return for press, photographic and cinematograph exhibition rights. Hurley was an essential part of the deal, as his Mawson film and an exhibition of his photographs had made a strong impression in Britain. Shackleton's aim was to cross Antarctica via the South Pole, from the Weddell Sea to the Ross Sea. His ship the *Endurance*, however, became stuck fast in the pack-ice within sight of land, before the expedition proper could begin, and what had been planned as the last great journey of polar exploration turned into an epic of survival. Hurley recorded all that he could (naturally, during the polar winter when there was total darkness he was unable to film at all), enlivening the necessarily static nature of a ship trapped in the ice with plenty of shots of the expedition's dogs, certain to be popular with audiences back home. He also recorded the death throes of the *Endurance*, capturing the precise moments when her masts and yards cracked and collapsed.

Frank Hurley.

What happened next says much about both Hurley and Shackleton. As the ship finally started to sink beneath the ice, Shackleton ordered that all but the most essential gear and supplies be left behind onboard, as they prepared to set out on foot. This included all of Hurley's cine film and photographic plates, Shackleton therefore abandoning the very artefacts whose financing had enabled the expedition to take place. There was an immediate logic to Shackleton's decision but not a long-term one. The attempt to continue across the ice by dragging sledges and boats soon proved impractical and they stopped within easy reach of the ship. Hurley resolved to rescue his work. The photographic plates and cine film were held in hermetically sealed tins within the ship's now submerged refrigerator and Hurley 'bared from head to waist' probed beneath three feet of 'mushy ice' in the hold to retrieve his films.

Initially, this heroic act was greeted with anger by Shackleton. Hurley reminded him of the commercial value of his work and a compromise was reached. Together they made a selection of 120 photographic plates, smashing the other 400 on the ice to avoid entirely the temptation to keep them all. Hurley thus kept with him these surviving plates, his developed cine film (some 5,000 feet), a pocket still camera and three spools of unexposed film. His cine camera and all other photographic equipment were left on the ship. Hence Hurley's film record ended with the sinking of the *Endurance*. The remainder of the expedition – the months spent drifting on ice floes, the crossing in three boats to Elephant Island, the start of Shackleton's boat journey to South Georgia and Shackleton's eventual rescue of his men – all of this Hurley had to record with the little photographic still film he had with him; and, of course, since Hurley remained with the party on Elephant Island, he could not record the voyage to South Georgia at all. This made the resultant film record

Hurley filming the bow of the trapped *Endurance*.

something of an oddity. However, what most concerned the film's backers when Hurley arrived in London, in November 1916, was that he had no film of Antarctic wildlife. As had been proved by earlier polar films, especially Ponting's of Scott's expedition which Hurley saw and greatly admired, what especially drew the public were quaint scenes of animal life. In the middle of a world war (in which he would afterwards serve with distinction as an official photographer and cinematographer in Palestine and on the Western Front) Hurley was therefore quickly sent back to South Georgia to film the essential animal scenes and provide other moving pictures to fill the unavoidable gaps in his cinematic narrative.

Shackleton resolved to make no profit from his adventures until the war had finished and so Hurley's films were not shown to the public until December 1919. That was when Shackleton's book *South* was published and he began a series of twice-daily lectures, lasting until May 1920, with Hurley's film as accompaniment, at the Philharmonic Hall in London. The experience of reliving the failure of his plans and the sinking of his ship, there on the big screen twice a day, can only have been painful for Shackleton, but debts had to be paid. The film, also entitled *South*, was never given a normal cinema release in Britain but it was later shown in other European countries. In 1920 it was released in Australia as *In the Grip of the Polar Ice*, where Hurley lectured to it as it toured the country with outstanding success. The film was reissued with a soundtrack in 1933 (including additional footage taken by Hubert Wilkins on Shackleton's later *Quest* expedition) under the title *Endurance: The Story of a Glorious Failure*, with a dignified commentary provided by Frank Worsley, captain of the *Endurance*.

The films of Herbert Ponting and Frank Hurley have enjoyed a pre-eminence in polar cinematography on account of the story of the expeditions themselves, the outstanding quality of the photographic work in extreme conditions, and the finished quality of the feature-length documentaries that resulted. It also needs to be pointed out that the haunting qualities of the still photographs that both Ponting and Hurley took alongside the cine film have enhanced the aura of their moving picture record. There were, however, other Antarctic film records made during the classical era of exploration, between Borchgrevink in 1898 and Shackleton's final expedition in 1921.

It is not widely known, for instance, that Amundsen's successful Norwegian expedition, which beat Scott to the Pole, was also filmed. Expedition member Kristian Prestrud operated the cine camera at the main base, while Amundsen's brother, Leon, appears to have filmed earlier scenes. The surviving footage shows Amundsen's ship *Fram* sailing southwards, scenes of daily life on board, the first icebergs and the approach to the ice shelf, whales in the Bay of Whales, and scenes of life at the Framheim base camp. Prestrud himself recorded that he also filmed Amundsen and his successful polar party starting out, while Amundsen wrote that his last sight of the companions he was leaving behind was of Prestrud operating the cinematograph, gradually disappearing beyond the horizon. The scene must have borne an eerily close resemblance to Ponting's shot of Scott and his team, likewise passing into the distance, never to return.

The Amundsen films appear not to have been made up into a finished documentary but were certainly exhibited in Britain at the same time as Ponting's, since they were included in lectures Amundsen gave in November 1912. But as with Dr Eric Marshall on Shackleton's *Nimrod* expedition, a member of the party chosen for other skills had been handed the filming chores, rather than the duty being given to an acknowledged expert, which made all the difference to Scott in 1910 and Shackleton in 1914.

The Kino camera used by Amundsen and his party on the *Fram* expedition.

The only other cinematographer of ability to film in the Antarctic at this time was George Hubert Wilkins. Wilkins too was an Australian, who came to Britain as a newsreel cameraman and filmed the Balkan War of 1913. He joined the Arctic expedition of Vilhjalmur Stefansson in 1913–16, before working with Frank Hurley as an official war photographer on the Western Front in 1918. Wilkins next found himself filming the misbegotten and amateurish Cope expedition to British Graham Land in 1920 (a short film, *Antarctica: On the Great White Trail South* survives), before he was selected as cinematographer to Shackleton's half-hearted *Quest* expedition of 1921. After Shackleton died of a heart attack at South Georgia on the outward journey, Wilkins had the impossible task of creating an expedition documentary with its central figure dead before the first reel was over. The resultant *Southwards on the 'Quest'* is predominantly a survey of animal life on South Georgia and, in its journeyman images, reveals Wilkins not to have been in the same filmic class as Hurley or Ponting.

Wilkins was an adventurer rather than an artist. He would later make his name (and earn a knighthood) conducting the first flights over the Arctic and Antarctica and becoming, in 1929, the first person to film Antarctica from the air – footage which was featured in newsreels. With Shackleton's death, however, the classical or heroic age of Antarctic exploration came to an end. One last film connected with Shackleton is worth noting. Sound films only came into regular production in the late 1920s but there were earlier experiments and, in 1921, just prior to his final expedition, Shackleton was filmed speaking about his plans by cameraman Arthur Kingston for the H. Grindell Matthews sound film system. The film has not survived.

Filming in the Antarctic of course continued beyond the time of Amundsen, Mawson, Scott and Shackleton. Commander Richard Byrd's flights to the North Pole (1926) and South Pole (1929) were both filmed by Pathé newsreel cameramen, Willard van der Veer and Bob Donohue in the Arctic and van der Veer and Joseph T. Rucker in Antarctica, for a film released as *With Byrd at the South Pole* in 1930. Frank Hurley returned to the scene, filming Douglas Mawson's 1929 Antarctic expedition (in Scott's refurbished vessel, *Discovery*) for a film eventually released as *Southward-Ho with Mawson!* Hurley filmed again with Mawson in 1930–31 but

'A meal on the march'; a still from Ponting's film *90° South*, posed for the cameras *en route*.

became irritated at the short time spent on land. He complained, 'we spent only 36½ hours on the Antarctic continent. To expect me to make a film of the Antarctic in such short time is ridiculous'. Nevertheless, *Siege of the South* (which incorporated footage from the earlier film) duly followed and Hurley's cinematography in it is thought by many to be the finest of all his Antarctic work.

The expedition film was then clearly dying out as a genre and what was to become an alternative use of cine film was shown during the 1934–37 British Graham Land Expedition, headed by John Rymill. The extensive film record, some 13,000 feet of 35mm film taken by Launcelot Fleming, was never edited into a would-be commercial film release but simply existed as a form of scientific documentation with an edited video version produced some fifty years later.

Commander Byrd and his team had filmed the South Pole from the air, but a film camera did not arrive at the Pole itself until the Commonwealth Trans-Antarctic Expedition of 1955–58 led by Vivian Fuchs and Edmund Hillary, which the cameras now filmed in colour. The expedition was covered in two atmospheric and well-edited documentaries, *Foothold on Antarctica* (1956), covering the expedition up to the setting up of the base camp, and *Antarctic Crossing* (1958), filmed by George Lowe and Derek Wright, which covered the successful crossing of the continent that had been Shackleton's too-grand ambition.

Thereafter television takes over and the remote becomes familiar. Now David Attenborough has offered us the *Life in the Freezer* series, with wildlife cinematography vastly superior to the pioneering efforts of Ponting and Hurley, and Michael Palin can bring the South Pole to millions in their living rooms, as he did at the conclusion of his popular television series *Pole to Pole*. The original footage of Hurley and Ponting has been regularly recycled in television documentaries, perhaps most notably in the BBC's excellent exploration series based around archival film, *Travellers in Time*. And we need not even wait for the television schedules to bring the South Pole to us. There is now a web camera positioned at the Automated Astrophysical Site-Testing Observatory (AASTO) at the Pole, delivering constant, live images from the bottom of the world for anyone who cares to click on. The struggle is over but the still and moving images of Hurley and Ponting of the great white silence endure (and the silence of the original films only adds to the awe), enhancing the legends and entrancing us every time they are shown. As Kathleen Scott said of Ponting's work in her introduction to his book, 'the beauty and wonder of them never varies'.

Notes

South and *90° South* are available on video from the British Film Institute (BFI). The BFI's National Film and Television Archive preserves these titles and other versions of the Scott and Shackleton films, including Ponting's *The Great White Silence*, recently fully restored. It also preserves *Antarctica: On the Great Trail South*, *Southwards on the 'Quest'*, the British Graham Land Expedition 1934–37 films, *Foothold on Antarctica* and *Antarctic Crossing*. Frank Hurley's *Home of the Blizzard* and *Siege of the South* are preserved by ScreenSound Australia. The film of Amundsen's expedition is held in the National Library, Rana, Norway. The AASTO webcam can be accessed at: http://bat.phys.unsw.edu.au/~aasto/

Endurance

Sir Ernest Shackleton: 'The Boss' of the *Endurance* expedition.

Out of whose womb came the ice? And the hoary frost of heaven, who hath gendered it? The waters are hid as with a stone, and the face of the deep is frozen.

Job 38: 29-30 (extract carried by Shackleton in the *James Caird*)

Shackleton arrived in London on 14 June 1909 after turning back from the South Pole, to a fanfare of public welcome. Getting within 100 miles was considered a tremendous achievement and the press rose to the occasion. Shackleton encouraged and basked in their attentions with interviews and quotable quotes. He was also a splendid lecturer and skilfully played to every audience available, including Edward VII at Balmoral. The King put him on a par with Scott by raising him to CVO and he became a national celebrity, much in demand.

He was also deeply in debt but most of his immediate problems were solved when the government added to its own pre-election popularity with a retrospective grant of £20,000 to meet *Nimrod* expenses. The expedition had cost less than half of Scott's for greater apparent results and had not needed naval rescue. Shackleton had already started to write his account of it in New Zealand but was aware of his literary limitations. He engaged Edward Saunders, an excellent journalist there, to come to London as his amanuensis, to whom he dictated the story for editing and polishing as *The Heart of the Antarctic.*

It appeared in November 1909, the month when Shackleton was also knighted in the Birthday Honours, and was hailed as 'book of the season'. Notwithstanding his shady brother, soon to be bankrupted and jailed for fraud, and his own erratic course in business matters, the Anglo-Irish outsider had reached a point scarcely less challenging than the Pole itself – a place in the heart of the English establishment. He also undertook a strenuous but profitable lecture programme throughout Britain, then to Europe in January 1910, where he entranced both the Kaiser in Berlin and the Tsar at St Petersburg. Previously in Oslo, Amundsen and the Norwegians honoured him for his achievement and courage in turning back with the Pole so nearly in his grasp. America followed from March, though more with the intention of raising funds for a new expedition with Mawson to explore west of Cape Adare. His success soon cleared his main *Nimrod* debts and Shackletonian charisma warded-off various smaller obligations, in some cases indefinitely.

But like Scott, Sir Ernest could not bear to be without a new project when the Americans were reportedly reaching the North Pole, the Germans and Scott himself preparing for the South. His own plans, however, were partly based on other business speculations which collapsed in the

'Return of the sun'; *Endurance* frozen in the ice, 1915.

downturn of confidence following Edward VII's death in May 1910. As Mawson and others found, Shackleton the polar leader was one thing, Shackleton the business partner another. When he obtained a £10,000 donation that Mawson believed was for the new project, it vanished to meet old commitments. Although Shackleton engineered replacement funds, their partnership did not survive and Mawson sailed in the *Aurora* without him.

When Scott left London to join *Terra Nova* in July 1910, Shackleton was among those who saw him off. The final phase of the 'heroic age' of polar exploration was beginning but Shackleton was left behind; frustrated, restless, unfit and with his private life unravelling. Emily was devoted and loyal but Shackleton was ill-adapted to domesticity and had always been attractive to women, which was part of his success in raising funds. He had an intense and longstanding friendship with Elspeth Beardmore, wife of William after whom the glacier was named. He now began a love-affair with Rosalind Chetwynd, an American who was divorced from her baronet husband and who later became an actress. While he still remained firmly attached to Emily in many ways this strange new relationship ('Rosa' was supported by another rich admirer) was to last for the rest of his life.

When Amundsen's arrival in the Ross Sea to challenge Scott became known in England in March 1911, Shackleton refrained from criticism of it. Amundsen's success at the Pole aroused his frank public admiration and his restraint from comment on Scott's failure and death was similarly notable, when news of these broke in February 1913. This contrasted with widespread British denigration of Amundsen and the spontaneous public grief over Scott. That Britain had been beaten was something Shackleton regretted. That Scott had not succeeded was a private compensation, not least when *Scott's Last Expedition* was published in late 1913 and had clearly been edited to put the disaster and its causes in the best possible light.

However, while attainment of the Pole had now closed one door, it had left open a last possibility for Antarctic achievement. Also seeing Scott off in 1910 was Oberleutnant Wilhelm Filchner of the German General Staff in Berlin who was planning an expedition to cross Antarctica from the Weddell Sea – a far more dangerously ice-infested bight than the relatively open Ross and one that had already crushed Larsen's *Antarctica* in 1903. He and Scott discussed the possibility of meeting at the Pole and exchanging men to make it a double crossing from both directions. The scheme was fantasy in the light of events but Filchner did sail in the *Deutschland* and was the discoverer of both the southern extent of the Weddell and the ice-shelf on its eastern side that now bears his name. There he also found a possible landing point at Vahsel Bay, named after the captain of his ship who died during the voyage. Filchner in fact got no further than the coast and had another narrow escape through being trapped in the Weddell's drifting pack-ice for nine months. However, his plan had revived

Shackleton's earlier idea of an Antarctic crossing, clarified the actual distance involved – about 1,500 miles as the crow flies – and indicated a potential landing site at the head of the Weddell Sea.

On 29 December 1913, having already briefed King George V and obtained a secret offer of £10,000 in government 'match-funding' from the Chancellor, Lloyd George, Shackleton announced he would be organizing an 'Imperial Trans-Antarctic Expedition'. It would be the longest sledge journey yet attempted and, in the words of *The Times*, would 're-establish the prestige of Great Britain … in Polar exploration'.

The plan was in fact based on one of his friend, the Scottish explorer William Bruce, though considerably modified. This time Shackleton intended to take two ships: one would land him at Vahsel Bay with the crossing party, the other would take a second group to McMurdo Sound to lay supply depots along the old Beardmore route to the Pole. Shackleton planned to make the crossing in 100 days, using dogs of which he ordered a hundred. The principle was sound and worked spectacularly well in the Fuchs-Hillary crossing of 1957–58. But even then, with the advantages of greater knowledge and mechanized transport, it took 99 days, by a route of just over 2,000 miles. On the eve of World War I nothing was known of the terrain between the Weddell and the Pole, and even Amundsen, with dog and ski expertise far beyond Shackleton's, had only averaged 16 miles a day on his polar journey of some 1,600 miles. As regards skis, Amundsen personally persuaded Shackleton that they were indispensable to survival but though he did some prior practice in Norway while testing equipment, including motor sleds, he still barely understood their potential. The eccentric Royal Marine, Captain Thomas Orde-Lees – another Anglo-Irishman and the only competent skier of the party – was amazed when, with his polar trek already abandoned, Shackleton expressed surprise at how fast he could ski and how useful it would have been. Orde-Lees wondered 'why he had not come to this conclusion long before and had

Left to right: Frank Wild; George Marston, a pre-departure publicity photograph in furs which were not taken on the *Endurance* expedition; Tom Crean with some of the puppies born on the *Endurance* expedition.

not insisted on every man ... being able at least to move on ski at a modest five miles an hour'.

In short, the whole thing was another visionary project launched with all Shackleton's impressive plausibility and talent for improvisation. The funds he needed were raised by his usual intricate manoeuvres, including £10,000 from Dudley Docker of the BSA Company, the government's £10,000 and an unconditional £24,000 donation from Sir James Key Caird, a Scottish jute millionaire. The press was enthusiastic and the scheme caught a tide of patriotic aspiration to achieve some national compensation in return for Scott's heroic defeat. Winston Churchill, First Lord of the Admiralty was among the sceptics ('Enough life and money has been spent on this sterile quest') and Orde-Lees was the only naval officer allowed to come. Scott had obtained analyses of provisions for the *Discovery* expedition from a government chemist. Shackleton opened up new ground in getting proactive scientific advice on nutrition from the War Office, and recruited a couple of army officers, including Philip Brocklehurst's brother, though the outbreak of World War I stopped them sailing.

Even war did not stop Shackleton, though it was a close-run thing. As with *Nimrod*, the whole expedition was put together in seven months. When he announced it, he already had his most loyal *Nimrod* follower, Frank Wild, on the strength again – this time to be second-in-command, which he had recently been under Mawson – and also George Marston, the artist in *Nimrod*. Round them a host of volunteers presented themselves and the crew of 27 finally assembled included some hardened Antarctic veterans: the third officer Alfred Cheetham had been in *Morning*, *Nimrod* and *Terra Nova* and Tom Crean in both *Terra Nova* and *Discovery*. The scientists like the physicist Reginald James , the geologist James Wordie, the meteorologist Leonard Hussey and the biologist Robert Clarke were all newcomers, as was the New Zealander Frank Worsley, who was to be the captain of Shackleton's ship, *Endurance*. He was to prove a gifted navigator and boat handler. The other important antipodean was Frank Hurley, the Australian photographer, with whom Shackleton already had a business partnership. Intrepid, practically ingenious and professionally gifted, he had just been south with Mawson. Even though most of his images were to be lost in *Endurance*, what he saved makes Shackleton's expedition the most strikingly recorded of the period. There were two doctors, Alexander Macklin and James McIlroy – both Ulstermen of an adventurous streak, the former also a sailor – and several hard-case seamen, notably George Vincent, who was disrated as bos'un for his bullying manner, and Harry McNeish, an expert but obstinately difficult shipwright and carpenter, who brought his cat. It was, once more, a disparate crew that only Shackleton's personality and the sterling reliability of Wild – a pillar of strength to all, including 'the Boss' – were to hold together.

Endurance herself was a new and untried wooden auxiliary barquentine of 300 tons, built in Norway as the *Polaris,* for 'arctic tourism', though this scheme collapsed: one of its principals had been Adrien de Gerlache. Shackleton bought her advantageously and also Mawson's *Aurora* (already in Tasmania), which was to be commanded by Aeneas Mackintosh, second-mate of *Nimrod*, to take the depot party to the Ross Sea.

At her own request the widowed Queen Alexandra visited *Endurance* in London just before she sailed on 1 August 1914. Austria had already declared war on Serbia and within days the dominoes of European alliances had fallen bringing in Germany, Russia, France and Britain. Shackleton's two army men and his original first officer went off to war but when the Admiralty declined his formal offer of both *Endurance* and her crew for war service, she made good her departure under Worsley's command, with mixed feelings among all concerned. The dogs, sixty-nine in all, were collected in Buenos Aires where both Hurley and Shackleton both joined by steamer. Shortly after leaving, Shackleton had one of his mysterious bouts of illness (which were to become more frequent during the venture). They also found a stowaway, Percy Blackborrow, who had been brought on board there by confederates in the crew, who feared they were short-handed. Shackleton first bawled him out then engaged him as steward. He proved an asset and was to have the dubious distinction of surviving an operation in appalling conditions on Elephant Island to remove frostbitten toes. *Endurance* then headed south for the unknown south-eastern shore of the Weddell Sea via the staging post of Grytviken, the Norwegian-run whaling station on South Georgia, from which she sailed on 5 December 1914.

The Weddell Sea as far south as the Ronne-Filchner ice-edge is an open bight some 950 miles deep on the western side, where it is enclosed by the Antarctic Peninsula, and about 500 to the east, at which point it is over 1,200 miles across. South Georgia is 1,500 miles due north of Vahsel Bay and Shackleton's route took him eastward, passing through the South

Percy Blackborrow and 'Mrs Chippy', McNeish's tom-cat, which was eventually put down with all the dogs.

Left to right: Reginald James, the physicist; Alexander Macklin and James McIlroy, the doctors.

'The way to the lead'. Several lines of ice cairns were thrown up, linked with cable, to serve as guidance back to the ship during blizzards.

One of the dogs.

Sandwich Islands before entering the pack-ice on 11 December in latitude 59° 28' south.

This is what he had been trying to avoid for as long as possible by keeping east but it was an appalling year in terms of the northerly limit of the summer pack. Ice in the Weddell Sea forms and lasts irrespective of season and moves in a slow clockwise motion driven by a prevailing current and south-easterly wind, within the western confinement of the Antarctic Peninsula. Ships caught in it are trapped for a long time and risk being crushed in a vast mill as the ice splits and grinds its way, under increasing pressure, west and northward up the Peninsular coasts of Palmer and Graham Land. This was to be the delayed fate of *Endurance* when on 19 January 1915 she finished her long eastward arc and stuck fast in the pack in latitude 76° 30' south, with the peaks above Vahsel Bay in sight but some 80 miles further on and to the east. The ice itself carried her further south to 76° 58' on 21 February but then, locked immovably in the floe, she had been swept past the Bay and begun the inexorable drift north on an erratic, slow and uncontrollable course. By the middle of March, Shackleton knew his Antarctic crossing was impossible. The best they could hope for – like de Gerlache, Bruce and Filchner before him – was that *Endurance* would survive the pressures and, perhaps a year later and 1,000 miles further north, escape when the pack broke up. In the meantime 'he showed one of his sparks of real greatness' wrote Macklin. 'He did not rage at all, or show outwardly the slightest sign of disappointment; he told us simply and calmly that we must winter in the Pack; explained its dangers and possibilites; never lost his optimism, and prepared for Winter'.

On the Ross Ice Barrier meanwhile, a now pointless saga of achieve-

Ice build-up on the deck of *Endurance*.

ment and suffering was also unfolding. *Aurora* had been fitted out with great difficulty by Mackintosh in Sydney, for money Shackleton had promised had not appeared. She sailed in ill-equipped confusion with an even more mixed and motley crew of twenty-eight than *Endurance* and the remainder of Shackleton's dogs, which had been shipped from England. Of the landing party of nine, only Mackintosh and Ernest Joyce, also from *Nimrod*, had any sledging experience and the former was to prove sadly inadequate as an expedition leader. They were in fact so poorly prepared and funded that they had to use Scott's old huts at Cape Evans and Hut Point and had no proper sledging rations. None the less, a party consisting of Mackintosh, Joyce, and Frank Wild's brother Ernest, who shared many of his sterling qualities, managed to lay a depot at 80° south on 20 February 1915 in preparation for Shackleton's arrival via the Pole. When they got back to Cape Evans on 2 June, after a terrible journey which killed many of their unacclimatized dogs, they found that *Aurora* had been blown from her exposed moorings there and out to sea, leaving them stranded. Mackintosh had foolishly not unloaded all the equipment and supplies immediately and these were still on board.

Shackleton also bore part of the blame. He had given strict orders to prevent the ship being iced in, like *Discovery*, at Hut Point but in trying to avoid this had indirectly ensured her equal entrapment out of reach, in the pack-ice of the Ross Sea. She would be 700 miles north of Cape Evans when she escaped in March the following year and in a condition that forced her

to make direct for New Zealand. The depot-laying party would only see her again, with Shackleton on board, when she finally returned to rescue them in January 1917. Until then they were entirely on their own, with only the stores that Teddy Evans had wisely left for later users at the end of Scott's second expedition and what they could kill, both for the pot and for fuel in the form of blubber. Fortunately Evans's cache included pemmican and other sledging supplies.

In January 1916 they made another gruelling, epic journey with their last few dogs to lay a depot for Shackleton's still-expected party at the foot of the Beardmore Glacier, 360 miles to the south. Its return leg was strangely parallel, in terms of the route, deprivations and conditions, to the one that killed Scott – and also a tragedy of wasted life given that Shackleton would never come.

Mackintosh's command had proved a catalogue of misjudgements. He finally collapsed from scurvy and had to be left alone, with three weeks food, for later rescue. Joyce had then already taken over and got all but one of the others, weak from malnutrition and exposure, back to Hut Point. The fatality was the Revd Arnold Spencer-Smith, incidentally the first clergyman in Antarctica. He had also developed severe scurvy and was dragged uncomplainingly on a sledge for over 300 miles before dying of heart failure two days from home. Joyce, Ernest Wild and Richards rapidly rescued Mackintosh but in May he and another of the Beardmore party, Victor Hayward, perversely decided to return to Cape Evans over the sea-ice before it was entirely safe. They had hardly left when a blizzard set in, the ice broke up and they were not seen again. Shackleton never lost a man but for the magic to work he had to be there in person.

Both *Endurance* and *Aurora* carried wireless equipment, the first exploration ships to do so: *Endurance* never managed to raise another station from the Weddell Sea. *Aurora* did finally make contact with Australia after her release from the ice in 1916. The technology that might have changed the course of events was there but was not advanced enough to have done so.

Frozen in

I think Sir Ernest is the real secret of our unanimity. Considering our divergent aims and difference of station it is surprising how few differences of opinion occur.

Thomas Orde-Lees

In the *Endurance* the main enemies were now uncertainty and boredom. Initially the ship was safe and Shackleton took steps to make his men as comfortable as possible, moving accommodation to the hold, which was warmer, and transferring the dogs to igloo kennels on the ice. Looking after them and practising with dog teams became one of the main general occupations, as was care of the various pups that appeared.

Football in the pack-ice.

Shackleton remained unflinchingly optimistic throughout. Backed especially by the solid and much-liked Wild, he skilfully minimized tensions among a crew which included uneducated seamen, unworldly academics, and the oddball Orde-Lees who used a bicycle on the ice and became something of a butt, though also a diligent store-keeper and a perceptive observer. People were left to get on with their own work, in the ship, in scientific observations or dog-minding, but he insisted on such things as punctuality at meals and maintaining social intercourse and common amusements – helped for example by Hussey, who played the banjo (it was to survive the whole saga, preserved as 'vital mental medicine' on Shackleton's order). He could control a degree of horseplay, which he often led: he was tactful, understanding, cheerful and although 'expert at nothing in particular... easily master of everything', according to Orde-Lees. Where Scott's anxieties had manifested themselves in silence and outbursts of temper, Shackleton – except when crossed on his known likes and dislikes – showed none, and he commanded an extraordinary degree of trust among his very mixed party.

Their prospects, however, were not good. One of the books on board was Otto Nordenskjöld's *Antarctic*, in which Carl Larsen told how his ship had been crushed in 1903, in the area to which the ice was slowly moving *Endurance*. By the end of May it was less slow: the ship and the floe in which she was locked were travelling north at about 10 miles a day with the ice beginning to work and groan as the pressure against the unseen land to the west built up. By the end of July *Endurance* had a list to port, and a damaged rudder and internal structure, and was surrounded by ominous pressure ridges. Between then and October she suffered a series of squeezes as the floe broke up and then closed again around her.

Leonard Hussey and his banjo (opposite) signed by the expedition members.

Although steam was raised in the hope she might float clear it was only used to pump against the growing leaks, as the hull damage increased. This and further exhausting hand-pumping did no good: though strong, *Endurance* was not of a specifically ice-resistant design like *Fram* or *Discovery*. As the crisis came, with the ship now over to starboard, boats and equipment were hastily transferred to the ice and on the evening of 27

'Men in Vaudeville'. Midwinter celebrations, 22 June 1915.

October, after the stern-post and part of the keel were wrenched away, Shackleton ordered her abandoned. Their position was 69° 5' south, longitude 51° 30' west – over 500 miles north of where she had been frozen in. 'It must have been a moment of bitter disappointment to Shackleton', wrote the senior doctor, Macklin, ' ... but he shewed it neither in word or manner ... Without emotion, melodrama or excitement [he] said "ship and stores have gone – so now we'll go home". 'I think' he continued, 'it would be difficult to convey just what those words meant to us ...'.

Shackleton's initial plan was to march over 300 miles across the heavily broken terrain of the pack to Snow Hill, Nordenskjöld's old base on the Antarctic Peninsula, where he knew there were supplies, and thence westward overland to Wilhelmina Bay, known to be frequented by whalers. However, this idea was abandoned after three exhausting days of dragging only moved two of the boats a couple of miles. Shackleton instead set up what they called 'Ocean Camp' on another solid floe where they had stopped, to reconsider the options. They also brought up the third boat and returned to salvage more from the surreally tangled wreck of *Endurance*. This included Hurley's photographic negatives, which he rescued from the submerged ship's refrigerator, before selecting 120 of the best, destroying the others and abandoning most of his equipment. Kept

The *Endurance* forced up out of the ice by heavy pressure, 19 October 1915. *The James Caird* is the boat nearest the camera.

in hermetically sealed cases, these and the film he had shot were to survive all that followed. Apart from the awful possibility of spending another Antarctic winter camped where they were, they either had to wait until the ice broke up or took them close enough to land to make a dash for it without the boats. On 21 November the distant funnel of *Endurance* dipped and vanished as the ice gripping her relaxed. She sank rapidly by the head, the floe closing over her as if she had never been.

At Ocean Camp it became a new waiting game, something to which Shackleton was temperamentally ill-suited, and in conditions that could only get worse. Hurley proved ingenious, manufacturing a blubber stove out of an ash-chute from the ship and later another portable one for the boats, as well as flooring the tents with salvaged timber. The drift north-ward continued and became more easterly, making the only likely escape one by sea to Paulet Island (where Larsen had found refuge) or, far worse, into the open ocean which the boats were unlikely to survive. At the end of November Shackleton gave these the names of his three most sympathetic sponsors: the largest, the double-ended whaler, became the *James Caird*, the other two the *Dudley Docker* and *Stancomb-Wills*, after Janet Stancomb-Wills, another of the wealthy and generous ladies who supported him.

By 21 December they had drifted 140 miles north of where *Endurance* went down and were in a plain of hummocked, broken ice, mushy under the sun of Antarctic summer and with leads of water opening up. Partly to counter sinking morale, Shackleton decided to attempt another march towards the land, towing two of the boats. By 28 December they had

Portside of *Endurance* looking forward.

'The End'. *Endurance* crushed but still gripped by the ice, just prior to sinking.

travelled nearly 10 miles but only after Shackleton crushed an incipient mutiny led by McNeish, the carpenter, who refused to continue on the fourth day's march. The first serious challenge to his authority, it arose partly from the personal grievances of McNeish and the foremast crew's traditional belief that, now *Endurance* had sunk, they would no longer be paid and had no duty to follow orders. Shackleton calmly persuaded them that he had full legal authority over them and that, of course, their pay continued. McNeish (whom he never forgave) he took aside and convinced that if his insubordination continued he would quite legally be shot.

'Look-out, Ocean Camp.' Shackleton stands on the right of the group.

They were stuck in their new position, 'Patience Camp', from New Year's Eve 1915 until the beginning of April 1916. Seals, which had been fairly plentiful, became short in mid-January, prompting Shackleton to save what meat there was for the men by having all except two teams of dogs shot. It would have been inevitable at some point but it did not help morale, already affected by the lack of food and its variety and the growing fear that they would be swept out of reach of land. At the start of February, when ice movement brought Ocean Camp back within 6 miles, the *Stancomb-Wills* was retrieved and by early March they were about 80 miles to the east of Paulet Island.

As the open ocean came closer the main fear was that the floe would crack under them or, as nearly happened, they would be run down by an iceberg driven by wind and current. On 9 March the ice was moving on ocean swell but though the boats were stowed to get away the opportunity to do so safely did not come. On the 23rd, 139 days after the loss of *Endurance* the distant peaks of Joinville Island at the tip of Graham Land were sighted about 40 miles off but still Shackleton delayed, rightly fearing the dangers of trying to launch boats in a sea full of heavy ice and unknown currents. By the end of the month they had drifted north, out of the Weddell Sea, into the marches of the Southern Ocean. The floe on which

they were camped was bound to disintegrate, food was increasingly short and the days too were shortening towards winter. The Peninsula was out of reach to the south-west and the only land within range to the north was Clarence or Elephant Island, parts of the South Shetland group over 100 miles away.

On 30 March the rest of the dogs were shot and eaten, and by 9 April the grinding of the pack had split and reduced the floe to the point that it had to be abandoned in dangerously ice-clogged sea conditions. At 1.30pm after drifting some 2,000 miles on their feet, all twenty-eight men embarked, and headed northward through a gauntlet of disintegrating and melting pack all around them. Shackleton commanded the *Caird*, and Worsley, the most skilled boat-handler, the *Dudley Docker*. Hubert Hudson, second officer of *Endurance* (who was weakening physically and mentally), was nominally in charge of the *Stancomb-Wills* but Crean effectively so. The *Caird* proved a good sailer, the other two extremely difficult and the conditions in all three were alarming and unpleasant. For the first two nights they hauled the boats out on a convenient floe, almost catastrophically on the first occasion, when the ice split, dropping one man in his sleeping bag in the sea and briefly separated Shackleton and the *Caird* from the rest. Thereafter they stayed in the boats, tied together at night, but three days from starting found that they had lost ground to the south and east rather than gained it northwards.

Shackleton then ordered a change of course to the south-west, back towards Graham Land, a decision that probably saved their lives. For on the following day, the 12th, the wind shifted to south-west allowing them to run before it towards Elephant Island. On the 13th they finally broke clear of ice but the next few days and nights were a catalogue of exhaustion, exposure, seasickness and continuous bailing, especially in the two smaller boats, with the *Caird* taking the unseaworthy *Stancomb-Wills* in tow to prevent her being lost. By the 15th, the seventh day of their voyage, with the peaks of Elephant Island before them, the *Docker* had become separated. Given their exhaustion and the appalling sea conditions right under the cliffs it was a near-miracle that both sections of the party managed to reach the leeward side of the Island and find the same landing place, one of very few, near Cape Valentine. That proved to be dangerous as a camping site and two days later, on the 17th, they moved to a stony, ice-covered beach 7 miles further along under a spit of rock which they called Cape Wild – honouring Frank Wild, who had soldiered on for thirty-two hours without sleep at the tiller of the *Caird*.

They had last been ashore in South Georgia sixteen months earlier, in early December 1914, and it was the first known landing on Elephant Island since 1830. A nearby glacier outfall promised water and a penguin rookery on the spit a food supply: of the sea elephants that gave the island its name, there was no sign. It was a barren, cold and unvisited rock, lost in a waste of ocean, but at least it was solid land.

James Caird
April–May 1916

Not a life lost and we have been through Hell.

Shackleton to his wife, 3 September 1916

On the afternoon of Saturday 20 May 1916, three bearded and filthily tattered figures walked into the Norwegian whaling station at Stromness on the north coast of South Georgia and were taken to the house of the manager, Thoralf Sørlle. He thought he recognized one but could not place him until he said 'My name is Shackleton ... Tell me, when was the war over?' Sørlle, who had met Shackleton at Grytviken in December 1914, welcomed them in but had to give a shocking answer: 'The war is not over. Millions are being killed ... The world is mad.' Fed, cleaned-up and rested, the three arrivals – the others being Worsley and Tom Crean – had an astonishing story to tell, though one which still had some way to run before its ending.

As soon as they had settled on the safe beach on Elephant Island, the 'directive committee' of Shackleton, Wild and Worsley agreed that their only hope was to seek rescue, since there was no chance of being found.

On 19 April Shackleton called for volunteers to accompany him in the *James Caird*, selecting Worsley for his proven skills, the tough and reliable Irishman, Crean, and the two most difficult lower-deck men, McNeish the shipwright and Vincent. The former might be essential to repair damage

On Elephant Island; the first drink and hot food for three days.

and Vincent, despite his faults, was a good seaman: taking them would also remove a source of trouble on the island. A final member was another cheerful Irish hand called Timothy McCarthy. Wild was left in charge at the new camp, with both the doctors (who were needed to take off Blackborrow's gangrenous left toes) and orders to try and reach Deception Island in the spring if rescue did not arrive. The two other boats were turned over and supported on heaps of stones, to form a hut under which all twenty-two men had to live, double-decked, with some sleeping on the boat thwarts above and the rest on the rocky, guano-caked beach below.

The freeboard of the 22 by 6½ ft *James Caird* had already been raised and a small foredeck added. Recycling the timber of a sledge, other pieces brought with them and a spare bolt of canvas, McNeish rapidly stretched a spray-proof but neither watertight nor solid deck over the rest of her, all except a small command hatch aft. He also strengthened her keel by lashing the mast of the *Stancomb-Wills* along it internally. Heavily ballasted with shingle from the beach packed in improvised bags, they sailed just after noon on Monday 24 April. The crew had only disintegrating reindeer sleeping bags, blankets and the clothes they wore, none waterproof. Their destination was South Georgia, to leeward of them in terms of prevailing wind and current across nearly 800 miles of the most stormy winter seas in the world.

Given that she should never have been in such waters the *Caird* proved

Elephant Island; launching the *James Caird* for the relief journey.

stable and safe, but with a motion that made everyone seasick. After a fair start the weather deteriorated to a Force 9 gale which obliged them to heave-to for a day but carried them on their way: by the 26th Worsley calculated they had covered 128 miles. Everything except sailing the boat was done below deck in an intensely cramped, wet, nauseous and uncomfortable environment. There was barely room to sit up properly, and with perpetual leakage through the canvas deck those below had to pump and bail almost continuously. The pump itself – another of Hurley's clever improvisations – also only worked with the boat already half bailed out. The sleeping area was in the bow, the driest part, though that was only relative, and cooking (done by Crean) was on a primus stove using ice fished from the sea where possible to eke out water. Shackleton had brought enough supplies for a month and, as a cardinal principle of care for his men, ensured everyone had frequent hot food or drinks and that a regular round of watches and rest was kept as far as possible. As before, his calm determination in the face of immediate danger and his solicitude for everyone were their psychological sheet anchor. Ever since *Nimrod*, he had dreamt of making such a boat journey but though now doing so had to confess that Worsley, not himself, was better qualified for the purpose and the better navigator.

By 29 April they had covered 238 miles but the following day were again forced to heave-to on their sea-anchor in wildly confused conditions

'Saved!'. Originally captioned as the rescue photograph, this image actually shows Shackleton's departure from Elephant Island in the *James Caird*.

and falling temperatures, of which the one advantage was that the deck canvas froze and at least stopped leaking. This, however, brought its own danger as the growing casing of ice on the upper works, a foot thick in places, made the boat unstable. Three times they risked lives crawling out onto the open deck to chip it off, soaking and freezing in the same breaking seas that formed it. On 2 May, still wallowing head to wind in icy conditions, the painter parted and they lost their sea anchor, a potential catastrophe since they could now only heave-to under sail, which was far more wearing.

Fortunately, 3 May saw the start of two days' fine weather but this soon changed to a north-westerly gale. At midnight on the 5th they were engulfed and nearly capsized by a massive sea, after which they hove-to again and spent the night frantically pumping and bailing. Vincent had by now become useless and McNeish was suffering badly; Crean and McCarthy remained cheerful and Worsley, as navigator, bore a huge burden, worsened by the rare occasions for taking sun sights in the poor conditions and with the boat 'jumping like a flea'. When on the 7th he made them 90 miles from South Georgia, they had only two days salt-contaminated water left and were beginning to suffer from thirst as well as exhaustion. Worsley had been aiming for the western end of the island, hoping to get round to the whaling stations on the north side but he could not be sure of his position. Fearing they might miss land altogether to the north, Shackleton decided to make for the uninhabited and practically unknown southern side. At 12.30 pm on the 8th, through thick weather, they briefly sighted the peaks of Cape Demidov to the west of King Haakon Bay and shortly afterwards, as the murk lifted, had the whole towering, iron-bound coast spread out across their track ahead.

By now it was too late to close the land with safety and Shackleton bore off for what was to be another terrifying night. By just after 6pm, in darkness, they were fighting a Force 10 storm blowing from west-north-west, with huge broken seas caused by the nearness to land. They none the less managed to claw off to the south before heaving-to again, pumping and bailing through the night. By noon the following day the wind had shifted to south-west at hurricane force, and was driving them towards the maelstrom lee-shore between King Haakon Bay and the fearsome peak of Annenkov Island just off the coast. Here again they were saved by Worsley's skills as he shifted their minimal sail to gain the maximum ground to the southward. After four hours, with the boat leaking through every seam from the straining and crashing, and the men bailing for their lives, they finally managed to clear the island by nightfall, with the weather subsequently moderating.

On the evening of the next day, 10 May 1916, exhausted, soaking and in agonies of thirst after a frustrating afternoon trying to beat into King Haakon Bay, they managed to scrape into a narrow cove just inside Cape Rosa, its south-eastern arm. Here they stumbled ashore to the welcome provided by a small spring of fresh water, seventeen days since leaving Elephant Island. 'It was', wrote Shackleton, 'a splendid moment.'

Four days rest in the cove, where there was shelter and driftwood for a fire, saw everyone dried out and their next move planned. The risks of trying to sail round to the north of the island were too great and Shackleton doubted whether the weakened McNeish and Vincent would survive the journey. He therefore intended to cross the icy peaks of the interior on foot, with Worsley – who had mountaineering experience in New Zealand and the Alps – and Crean. McCarthy would stay behind with the invalids, well supplied with rations and with game to be had: they had already been eating fresh albatross chicks and sea elephant.

Above the north end of the long bay they had seen a glaciated saddle which looked like an obvious way up. This was the route they took on 19 May, having sailed the *Caird* over to the north side on the 15th and upended her on a new stretch of beach to form a hut, at what they called 'Peggotty Camp'. The aim was to reach the permanent whaling station at Husvik, at the head of Stromness Bay, a direct distance of only about 20 miles. That was the theory. In practice, it was winter on a barren island of highly changeable weather with unmapped, glacier-coated central mountains of heights then unknown (up to 3,000 ft on average). Apart from being physically weak, they were inadequately dressed, with boots whose only grip was provided by inserting screws from the *Caird* in the soles. The only other equipment they had were compasses and an outline chart of the coast, a 50-foot length of rope and McNeish's short carpenter's adze to use as an ice-axe. They took three days supply of rations per man and a primus stove, but no sleeping bags: Shackleton planned to do the crossing in a single march, day and night, with minimum stops for rest and food and taking advantage of a full moon. The weather delayed the start but thereafter was almost freakishly fine, although very cold at night and sometimes misty.

Starting at 2 am they climbed and marched up over 1,000 feet across the dangerous glacial saddle and in about six hours were within sight of deserted Possession Bay, the most westerly of the long, regularly spaced fjords penetrating the north coast. Thereafter things became increasingly difficult as they had to regain height lost by descending too soon and pick their way east across a high ridge whose first three passes proved to have impossible reverse faces. As they used the adze to cut steps down the ice beyond the fourth, late on the 19th, the light began to fail and they risked using the coiled rope as a toboggan, careering down a 1,500-foot slope to avoid the greater danger of being trapped above in darkness. In the night they again lost the line of their route, descending on the western side of Fortuna Bay, the next along the coast, and having to climb up again to another jagged ridge. Near the top, after some 22 hours on the move, Shackleton allowed the others a brief sleep, himself keeping watch, before they went over the crest and could at last recognize the distant heights above Stromness. At 7 am on the 20th they heard the faint factory whistle from one of the whaling stations, though still some miles away.

To get round the head of Fortuna Bay they had a short but frightening final traverse, tied together, Shackleton again cutting their steps down a wall of ice with the risk of a slip from any of them catapulting all three into the sea far below. This led them down to a beach by mid-morning with one more 1,500-foot ridge to cross to reach Stromness, which Shackleton now judged an easier destination than Husvik. To their jubilation, Stomness Bay was in sight below by early afternoon. On the way down their last misdirection left them in a mountain stream with a soaking, 30-foot drop through the waterfall at the end of it using their rope, which at last proved its strength but was lost there. Thirty-six hours and nearly 40 miles after starting they walked into the whaling station at about 4 o'clock, 1,500 miles north of where *Endurance* had frozen in the pack-ice, and into a world which the slaughter of Flanders and Gallipoli had already changed forever.

Yelcho
May–August 1916

Do not let it be said that Shackleton has failed ... No man fails who sets an example of high courage, of unbroken resolution, of unshrinking endurance.

Roald Amundsen

The final scene of Shackleton's expedition was only played out in the following year, 1917, when he returned in *Aurora*, commanded by Captain John King Davis, to rescue the Ross Sea party. However the last act of the *Endurance* drama began as a fairly local matter, though with distant Royal Naval echoes intruding. On the night of their arrival Worsley slept aboard the whale-catcher *Samson*, manned by a Norwegian crew and already making her way out through a blizzard to fetch the men at King Haakon Bay, who did not initially recognize his cleaned-up form when he arrived. They returned to Stromness on Monday 22 May, bringing the *James Caird* with them, a gesture Shackleton greatly appreciated, (In 1922, after his death, the boat was presented to Dulwich College, his old school, where she can still be seen).

During their absence Shackleton was lent the use of an English steam whaler laid-up at Husvik, the *Southern Sky*, to mount a rescue of the men on Elephant Island. He, Worsley and Crean, sailed with her on 23 May under a Norwegian captain, Ingvar Thom, who happened to be available as his ship was in harbour, but they were stopped by thick sea-ice 70 miles short. Instead of returning to South Georgia, however, Shackleton diverted Thom to Port Stanley in the Falkland Islands, which had a cable station, and announced news of his escape to the world via the London *Daily Chronicle*, to which he was under commercial contract. The news broke in banner headlines on 31 May, the day the Battle of Jutland was fought. Thom then left and Shackleton found himself enjoying the hospitality of the Governor but with no ship available in Stanley to make another rescue attempt.

By this time, his supporters in London, including Ernest Perris, editor of the *Daily Chronicle*, had already been urging high-level official action over the vanished expedition. The Admiralty was understandably reluctant, both because of the war and having had enough of sorting out such messes in the recent past. However, an approach to Prime Minister Herbert Asquith and *Aurora*'s wireless signal to Australia on 24 March 1916 after her escape from the ice clinched the matter, even before Shackleton materialized to appeal for help two months later. The Navy fitted out *Discovery* for the task at Devonport. Lent free by the Hudson's Bay Company and under the command of a Dundee Ice Master, she departed from Plymouth in mid-August 1916, escorted by two armed trawlers, to be towed by a collier as far as Montevideo. Shackleton however was not prepared to wait, not least because the Admiralty showed no willingness to allow him to command the mission as he requested, only asking him to act in an advisory capacity. In the interim he was all the more determined to rescue his men himself.

Through the good offices of the Uruguayans, the next attempt to reach Elephant Island was made by their fisheries research trawler, *Instituto de Pesca No. 1*. This collected Shackleton, Worsley and Crean from Port Stanley on 16 June but returned them there after again being forced back

'Rescue'. The crew await rescue by Shackleton aboard the *Yelcho*. The smoke signal on the left of the photograph was added by Hurley after the event.

by ice, 20 miles from the Island.

With only the option of waiting for *Discovery* at Port Stanley, on 1 July the three men shifted their ground to Punta Arenas in Chile, on the Straits of Magellan. Here Shackleton quickly raised money from the British community and other admirers to charter a 75-ton schooner, the *Emma*, for his third attempt. They sailed on the 12th, towed part of the way by the Chilean navy tender *Yelcho*, but the voyage was otherwise more reminiscent of the pre-steam era. It was made largely under sail because of deficiencies in the *Emma*'s diesel engine and they were again stopped 100 miles short by ice. They then had to beat back against the prevailing westerlies, reaching Port Stanley on 3 August.

Shackleton was becoming desperately anxious for his men, with no prospect of *Discovery* arriving before late September and the distant Admiralty immovable that he would be nothing but a passenger. The Chileans again sent out the *Yelcho* to help him return *Emma* to Punta Arenas, where she arrived on 14 August with Shackleton again in doubtful health. There, his burning desire to rescue his men before the Royal Navy arrived persuaded both the local naval commander and his superiors in

Santiago to allow one last attempt using *Yelcho* alone. She was a small steel tug of about 150 tons, not in very good repair either structurally or mechanically and certainly not built for ice. Shackleton, Worsley and Crean sailed in her with a crew of Chilean volunteers on 25 August. The commander, Lieutenant Luis Pardo, obligingly allowed Shackleton his

The members of the *Endurance* expedition safe in Punta Arenas, Chile.

head to direct their movements and wisely left the navigation to Worsley.

This time there was no ice as they approached Elephant Island, only fog, through which Shackleton was allowed to close the land at some risk during the night of the 29th, increasingly anxious lest wind and current bring the ice back in. Worsley's navigation was again excellent but they nearly missed Cape Wild by approaching from the unfamiliar western side rather than the east. That was quickly resolved and at 1pm on the 30th they were lying off the spit in conditions almost alarmingly calm. Shackleton went off in a boat and found an excited and emotional party all well on shore, where they had almost given up hope. He superstitiously refused to land at all and insisted on immediate evacuation.

Wild had long made the party live in a state of readiness to move at short notice. Within an hour everyone was embarked, the remains of the camp and the *Endurance*'s last two boats were abandoned and the *Yelcho* headed fast for the open sea before her luck could turn. On 3 September 1916 they made a triumphant entry into Punta Arenas, cheered by Chileans and members of the English, German and Austrian communities alike, the war notwithstanding. With his thoughts now turning to how the world would react to his epic of survival snatched from the jaws of failure, and the story to be made of it, Shackleton had of course ensured they did not arrive without advance fanfare.

Voyages' end

The settee from Thoralf Sørlle's house at Stromness, on which Shackleton rested after his 36-hour crossing of South Georgia to seek rescue for his men.

The 'race to the South Pole' in the years before World War I involved more people, of many nationalities, than have appeared in this brief account of the three names that dominate British perception of it.

Scott, like Nelson, has been assured immortality in the British pantheon by the manner of his death. The fact that it occurred in what was popularly seen as a close-run if unsuccessful contest for a national goal, made him a British Imperial hero. Since then, and also like Nelson, the passing of Empire itself has prompted reconsiderations which have questioned Scott's competence, if not his tragic status.

Historical perspective of course makes it easy to criticize Scott. It does him greater justice to recognize that, far more than Amundsen or Shackleton, he was a conventional product of his background — English, Naval , Victorian, — and, to a degree, a casualty of its limitations as well as of any personal factors. Had he been different, as Amundsen was both as a Norwegian and in cast of mind, and Shackleton too as an unconventional, romantic adventurer, neither Markham nor his committee-men would have backed him. On the scientific front his expeditions achieved wide and important results: the scientific observations from Amundsen's southern

The cairn built over Scott's final resting place.

foray (setting aside those of *Fram*'s independent oceanographic survey) were very slight by comparison. However, Scott did not have the outlook, skills or competitive focus by which Amundsen beat him to the Pole, or the natural leadership gifts by which Shackleton achieved, or at least appeared to achieve, more in defeat than his practical failings and improvisations probably deserved.

One aspect of Scott, which should at least be noted, is the question of how far his temperament — introspective, sensitive and with both charm and notable literary gifts — may have been incompatible with the career he chose, or at least with the extreme circumstances into which it led him. There has been no scope to do more than hint at this here but, if such a contradiction has any substance, it would both deepen the nature of his tragedy and the respect due to the bravery with which he met his death.

That death, however, and the rationalization of pointless sacrifices in the 'Great War' so soon afterwards, put Scott beyond immediate criticism. Neither Amundsen nor Shackleton were so lucky. Nothing which either did afterwards matched, in the former's case, winning of the race to the South Pole and, in the latter's, his escape from it. Both had to live with anticlimax.

Although various delays and the War intervened, Amundsen continued to explore. He built a new ice-ship, the *Maud*, in which from July 1918 he began a seven-year attempt to accomplish his drift across the Arctic Ocean. Thanks to the vagaries of wind and current, however, *Maud* only succeeded in traversing its edges, through the North-East Passage (the second ship to do so) and Amundsen did not complete the full voyage himself.

During the war, aged 50, he had learnt to fly and despite personal bankruptcy and other difficulties he began a series of attempts to cross the North Pole by air in 1923. In 1925 he and his companions were nearly stranded after one of their two planes was damaged in a forced landing on the Arctic pack. The following year, however, Amundsen and the Italian, Primo Nobile, succeeded in flying over the North Pole from Spitsbergen to Alaska in the Italian-built airship *Norge*. The flight restored Amundsen's flagging reputation and public popularity but he then quarrelled with Nobile and others, and his last years were increasingly isolated and occupied with efforts to clear his debts. He was eventually successful but, unfortunately, the bitter tone of his autobiography did little to help, when it was published in 1927.

In 1928 Nobile made another flight to the Pole in the airship *Italia* but disappeared on the return. As a matter of honour, Amundsen rapidly became involved in the ill-co-ordinated rescue attempts, his name inducing the French government to provide a Latham flying-boat and crew for the purpose. With his pilot companion, Leif Dietrichson, and the French crew of four under Captain René Guilbaud, Amundsen took off from Trømso on 18 June 1928. They were never seen again. Wreckage found in the sea months later suggested they had made a forced landing and subsequently perished in circumstances that can only be imagined. For Amundsen it was a tragic but perhaps fitting end. Nobile was rescued by others.

Shackleton and his crew were welcomed as a heroes in South America in 1916. They finally parted at Buenos Aires and Shackleton made his way to join *Aurora* in New Zealand for the rescue of the Ross Sea party. They returned to Wellington on 9 February 1917, again to a considerable welcome. Shackleton's return to England in May, after lecturing in America, was notably quiet by comparison. He was already actively seeking a role in the War, aware of a degree of criticism for being so long absent from it 'messing about on icebergs', in one reported phrase.

Initially he was unsuccessful but between October 1917 and the spring of 1918 he was sent on a British propaganda mission to South America. In July 1918, after his return, Shackleton was gazetted temporary major in the army and became involved in a semi-commercial expedition to establish a British presence in Spitsbergen, in which Wild and McIlroy were also employed, the latter now invalided from the army through wounds suffered at Ypres. In August at Trømso, however, he was taken ill with what McIlroy thought was a heart attack but, as usual, resisted investigation.

From there he was suddenly called home to organize transport aspects of a new military mission to Murmansk. This outlasted the end of the war, becoming ongoing British support for the regional government against the

Bolshevik threat. Shackleton extended it into proposing schemes for local economic development which, had they worked out, would have provided him with a post-war future. Unsurprisingly, his return to England in March 1919 and the withdrawal of British forces later that year saw the whole effort collapse and the area fell to the communists.

His peacetime life again became a search for income, initially by a drudging round of lecturing on the *Endurance* expedition, from December 1919 to May 1920. As we have seen, this included providing a live commentary to Hurley's remakable silent film, *In the Grip of the Polar Ice*, twice a day at the Philharmonic Hall. Shackleton's book of the expedition, *South*, again ghosted by Edward Saunders, appeared to a good reception in December 1919. Shackleton gained nothing by it, having assigned the royalties to the heirs of one of his more unforgiving creditors, and he was never to clear many of his other *Endurance* debts. By this time his marriage was also one of form rather than substance and he was spending an increasingly rootless existence with his mistress, Rosalind Chetwynd, or otherwise on the move. He was also drinking and smoking too much, and visibly ageing.

Early in 1920 he began to say he wanted to see the polar regions again, forming plans for the Canadian Arctic in which he was offered backing by a wealthy former school friend, John Quiller Rowett. When Canadian support proved elusive, Rowett generously agreed to a vague alternative plan to circumnavigate Antarctica and fix the position of various ill-charted islands. In three months, Shackleton put together his last expedition in the 125-ton sealer *Quest*. For this he surrounded himself with old friends, a number of whom were still owed money from *Endurance* days: Wild, Worsley, Macklin, McIlroy and Hussey were among them, and new faces too. They sailed from London on 21 September 1921, via Plymouth, Madeira and Rio de Janeiro. Shackleton was now clearly in poor health, increasingly listless, nostalgic and a cause of concern to the doctors. At Rio he had a heart attack but again refused to be properly examined.

On 4 January 1922, a fine day turning into a wonderful evening, they were welcomed at Grytviken in South Georgia by old Norwegian friends. Shackleton had already confessed that he had no clear plans thereafter and McIlroy later recalled that, leaving Plymouth, the tolling of a bell-buoy had prompted him to remark 'That's my death knell'. On board *Quest* in the small hours of the following morning, 5 January, Macklin came to his urgent call and found him in the middle of another heart attack. As he had often done before, the doctor told him he would have to change his ways. 'You're always wanting me to give up things', said Shackleton, ' what is it I ought to give up?'. Macklin replied 'chiefly alcohol Boss, I don't think it agrees with you.'

Shackleton's grave on South Georgia.

It was their last exchange: Shackleton died within minutes, six weeks short of his forty-eighth birthday. With Hussey as escort, his body was sent home for burial but only got as far as Montevideo. There a message was received from Emily, always the forgiving and understanding wife, that her ever-restless husband should remain where his heart lay, in the Southern Ocean. On 5 March 1922, the remote way-station of his voyages became his final harbour when he was buried on South Georgia, in the Norwegian whalers' cemetery at Grytviken.

Old and New: January 2000
Photograph taken from Hut Point. The *Discovery* hut can be seen in the foreground with the McMurdo Station (1957-present) in the distance. Taken by Gerard A. Sellek during the National Science Foundation (USA) event BO-301.

Selected Biographies

Amundsen, Roald Engelbreth Gravning (1872–1928)

See chapter 4, (p. 55) and Voyages End, (p. 129)

Armitage, Albert (1864–1943)

Armitage was a cadet in HMS *Worcester* before joining the P&O line in 1886. In 1894 he was released to serve as navigator on the Jackson–Harmsworth expedition to Franz–Joseph Land in the Arctic where he remained for two and a half years. He returned to P&O in 1896, before being appointed navigator and second-in-command on the *Discovery* expedition in May 1900.

Atkinson, Edward Leicester (1882–1929)

After qualifying in 1906 at St Thomas's Hospital Medical School, Atkinson went on to serve at the Royal Naval Hospital, Haslar. He joined the *Terra Nova* expedition in 1910 as junior surgeon and parasitologist and led the search party that discovered Scott's body in November 1912. He was awarded the Albert Medal during World War I and had to retire from the Royal Navy at the age of 46 due to injuries sustained during the war.

Barne, Michael (1877–1961)

Michael Barne joined the Navy in 1893. He served as second lieutenant on the *Discovery* expedition. Barne attempted to organize his own expedition to the Weddell Sea after *Discovery*, but had to abandon the idea after failing to raise sufficient funds. Frostbite injuries to his hands prevented him from serving on the *Terra Nova* expedition.

Bernacchi, Louis (1876–1942)

A Tasmanian, Bernacchi had been one of the men to over winter at Cape Adare as part of the *Southern Cross* expedition in 1899. He joined the *Discovery* expedition as physicist and was responsible for seismic and magnetic research. His own colourful account, *The Saga of the Discovery*, was published in 1938.

Borchgrevink, Carsten Egeberg (1864–1934)

Borchgrevink was a Norwegian and childhood friend of Roald Amundsen. He travelled to Australia in 1888 and, after a variety of jobs, signed on as a crew member in the *Antarctic*, a Norwegian sealer, in 1894. During the voyage when a party landed at Cape Adare, Borchgrevink was one of the first men to set foot on Antarctica, in 1895. Inspired by his experience and determined to be the first man to winter on the continent, by 1899 Borchgrevink had raised sufficient funds from a British sponsor, Sir George Newnes, to return as leader of his own expedition aboard the *Southern Cross*. He successfully spent the winter of 1899–1900 at Cape Adare and travelled south by sledge to 78° 50' south – then the furthest south reached by man.

Bowers, Henry Robertson, 'Birdie' (1883–1912)

Born in 1883, descended from a Scottish seafaring family, Henry Bowers earned the nickname 'Birdie' because of his distinctive nose. In September 1897 he was enrolled as a cadet in HMS *Worcester* from where he entered the merchant service. In 1905 he left to join the Royal Indian Marine Service as a sub-lieutenant. He had read Scott's account of the *Discovery* expedition and had a lifetime fascination with polar exploration. He was recommended for the *Terra Nova* expedition by Sir Clements Markham and approved by his former commander in HMS *Worcester*. He died with Scott and Wilson on their return journey from the Pole.

Bruce, Wilfred Montagu (1874–1953)

Kathleen Scott's brother, Wilfred Bruce had served as a cadet in HMS *Worcester* before joining the merchant navy. He joined the *Terra Nova* expedition, supporting Meares in transporting dogs and ponies selected for the expedition from Vladivostock to New Zealand.

Campbell, Victor Lindsey Arbuthnot (1875–1956)

Victor Campbell served on the *Terra Nova* expedition where he was picked by Scott to lead what became the Eastern Party – later known as the Northern Party when they were put ashore at Cape Adare – the area originally explored by Borchgrevink. Known as 'the mate' or 'the wicked mate' Campbell and his five companions spent seven months of the 1912 winter in a 9x5ft ice cave, cut off from relief and lacking adequate equipment and rations. They then sledged the 200-mile journey back to Cape Evans only to learn that Scott and his four companions had died nine months earlier.

Cherry-Garrard, Apsley George Benet (1886–1959)

Selected by Wilson to join the scientific team on the *Terra Nova* expedition as assistant zoologist, 'Cherry' as he was known, travelled with Wilson and Bowers on their extraordinary winter journey to collect Emperor penguin eggs in 1911. His own fine account of the *Terra Nova* expedition, *The Worst Journey in the World*, was published in 1922. In it he showed his misgivings that, had he disobeyed his orders and travelled on beyond One Ton Depot to look for Scott's return sledging party, they might have been saved.

Colbeck, Lt William Robinson (1871–1930)

Colbeck was a Yorkshireman who sailed with Borchgrevink to Antarctica in 1898, one of only three British subjects on this largely Scandinavian-manned British Antarctic Expedition. He was one of those who reached Borchgrevink's 'furthest south' with him. He was also captain of the *Morning*, the relief ship sent to effect the release and rescue of the ice-bound *Discovery*.

Crean, Thomas (1876–1938)

Crean was born at Annascaul in County Kerry, Ireland. He joined the *Discovery* as an able seaman and his powerful build marked him as an excellent sledger. He went on to serve on the *Terra Nova* expedition from HMS *Bulwark* and was awarded the Albert Medal for saving the life of Teddy Evans. Crean then bought himself out of the Navy in 1912 in order to join Shackleton's *Endurance* expedition, during which he was one of the six who sailed to South Georgia in the *James Caird* and then crossed the mountainous island on foot with Shackleton and Worsley to find help at Stromness. He later returned to Annascaul to open a pub called 'The South Pole inn'. A man of extraordinary physical and mental toughness, Crean eventually died of appendicitis.

David, Sir T.W. Edgeworth (1858–1934)

Although Welsh-born and Oxford-educated, David's career is linked with Australia, where he became a geological surveyor in 1882 and Professor of Geology at Sydney University in 1891. He was particularly interested in past geological climates and was elected a Fellow of the Royal Society in 1900. After giving Shackleton much help with the *Nimrod* expedition he was invited to join it as Chief Scientist. He led the first ascent of Mount Erebus and it was his party that first located the South Magnetic Pole. He later rose to the rank of Lieutenant Colonel as a military tunnelling expert in World War I and was knighted in 1920, remaining a major figure in his scientific field throughout the Commonwealth until his sudden death in 1934.

Debenham, Frank (1883–1959)

Born in New South Wales, Debenham was selected by Wilson as a geologist for the *Terra Nova* expedition. 'Deb' as he was known, went on to found the Scott Polar Research Institute in 1925 with James Wordie and Raymond Priestley, becoming its first Director.

Evans, Edgar (1876–1912)

Born at Middleton in South Wales, 'Taff' Evans joined the Royal Navy in 1891. He was selected for the *Discovery* expedition and went on to become a physical training officer and naval gunnery instructor in 1904 before volunteering for the *Terra Nova* expedition. He died on the Beardmore Glacier on 17 February 1912, the first casualty of Scott's five-man Polar party.

Evans, Edward R.G.R. (1881–1957)

'Teddy' Evans joined the Royal Navy from the training ship HMS *Worcester* in 1896. In 1902 he convinced Sir Clements Markham that he should be appointed as second officer in the relief ship *Morning*, which found the *Discovery* in McMurdo sound. In 1910 he decided to form his own expedition to the South Pole but on hearing of Scott's plans, offered his services and joined the *Terra Nova* as second-in-command. He was instrumental in gathering support and funds for the expedition. He almost died from scurvy on the Ross Ice Shelf, but was saved by the actions of Petty Officers Crean and Lashly. He was to return to the Navy after the expedition to become a war-hero in command of the destroyer *Broke* and was created a Labour peer in 1946 as Admiral Lord Mountevans.

Ferrar, Hartley T. (1879–1932)

Hartley Ferrar replaced Dr J.W. Gregory, who had resigned, as geologist on the *Discovery* expedition. He discovered fossilized remains of early flora in Victoria Land.

Gerov, Dimitri (1888?–1932)

Born in Eastern Siberia, Gerov, (the English spelling of whose name varies considerably) supported Meares in selecting and then transporting the dogs purchased for the *Terra Nova* expedition from Russia to New Zealand and onward to the Antarctic. He joined the expedition as dog handler.

Gran, Tryggve (1889–1980)

Introduced to Scott by Fridtjof Nansen, Gran had planned his own expedition but was selected for the *Terra Nova* expedition because of his skiing expertise. He was a member of the search party that discovered Scott's tent. Later, Shackleton failed to persuade him to go on the *Endurance* expedition.

Hodgson, Thomas Vere (1864–1926)

In an interlude from his work as Director of the Marine Biological Association Laboratory in Plymouth, Hodgson joined the *Terra Nova* expedition as a biologist, being one of the two eldest members of the party.

Hussey, Leonard (1894–1965)

Hussey was meteorologist on the 1914 *Endurance* expedition. He was also a talented musician and entertained the men stranded on Elephant Island with songs and banjo playing.

Hurley, Frank (1886–1962)

Frank Hurley bought his first camera at the age of 17. He showed particular talent for landscape photography and set up a post-card business to exploit his skills. In 1910 he was asked by fellow Australian Douglas Mawson to accompany his Antarctic Expedition of 1911. Hurley created a remarkable range of images and also made the film *Home of the Blizzard*, the documentary which charts

Mawson's *Aurora* expedition of 1911–13. This was seen by Ernest Shackleton who then hired Hurley to join the *Endurance* expedition in 1914. As stills and cine cameraman, Hurley displayed great tenacity and determination while his ingenuity and early training as a metal-worker were also enormously useful. He returned to South Georgia in 1916 to shoot additional footage for his film, *South*, which was released in 1919.

James, Reginald (1891–1964)

James joined the scientific team on the *Endurance* expedition as a physicist.

Koettlitz, Reginald (1861–1916)

Koettlitz had volunteered to serve in the position of doctor on the Jackson–Harmsworth expedition to the Arctic in 1894. He received his appointment as senior surgeon and bacteriologist on the *Discovery* expedition in 1900. A rather serious figure, and the oldest member of the party, his companions gave him the nickname 'Cutlets'.

Lashly, William (1868–1940)

Born in Hampshire, Lashly served as Leading Stoker in the *Discovery*. His strength and dependable nature made him a natural success on the expedition. He went on to serve as an instructor at the Royal Naval College, Osborne, before volunteering for the *Terra Nova* expedition. With Tom Crean, he was awarded the Albert Medal for saving the life of Teddy Evans.

Lillie, Dennis G. (1884–1963)

Lillie was biologist on the *Terra Nova* expedition.

Markham, Sir Clements (1830–1916)

While in the Navy, Markham served on the 1850–51 expedition to search for the Arctic explorer Sir John Franklin. He was President of the Royal Geographical Society, 1893–1905, and a passionate advocate of Antarctic exploration, securing Scott's selection as leader for the 1901 *Discovery* expedition.

Marston, George (1882–1940)

Born in Southsea, Marston had trained to be an art teacher in London. He joined Shackleton's *Nimrod* and

Endurance expeditions as artist, recording events which would then illustrate the official accounts of the expeditions. After the *Endurance* expedition he went on to join the Rural Industries Board, of which he was Director from 1934 to his death in 1940.

Mawson, Sir Douglas (1882–1958)

One of Australia's greatest explorers, English-born Mawson was the geologist selected to join Ernest Shackleton's *Nimrod* expedition (1907–09). As a member of the scientific team he joined the ascent of Mt Erebus and the journey to the South Magnetic Pole. He went on to command the Australian Antarctic Expedition from 1911–14 aboard the *Aurora*. In 1912, Mawson was the sole survivor to return from a three-man, four-month expedition. He recounted this extraordinary story of survival against the odds in his book *Home of the Blizzard*, first published in 1915. He was knighted in 1914 and led the British, Australian and New Zealand Antarctic Research Expedition (BANZARE) in the *Discovery* in 1929–30 and 1930–31.

Meares, Cecil (1877–1937)

A traveller, adventurer and trader in the East, Meares was appointed by Scott in 1910 to buy dogs and ponies in Siberia and then transport them to New Zealand to join the *Terra Nova* expedition. He was the only experienced dog-driver among the British team and persuaded Dimitri Gerov to join the expedition when buying the dogs.

Murray-Levick, George (1877–1956)

Murray-Levick was senior surgeon on the *Terra Nova* expedition and one of the Northern Party which spent the winter of 1912 living in an ice cave when they became stranded. He also studied the Adélie penguin colonies at Cape Adare and his book *Antarctic Penguins* (1914), was the standard work on the subject for many years.

Nansen, Fridtjof (1861–1930)

In 1893, Nansen, the Norwegian Arctic explorer and marine biologist had sailed to the Arctic on board the specially designed *Fram*, hoping to drift across the North Pole. Although unable to reach his final destination, the expedition provided much new information about the Arctic Ocean, proving that sea surrounded the Pole. He published his account of the expedition in *Farthest North*, first published in English translation in 1897. He became an Ambassador for Norway and a respected Polar authority, advising Scott, Amundsen and Shackleton alike.

Oates, Captain Lawrence Edward Grace (1880–1912)

Known as 'Titus' or 'the Soldier', Oates was an expert horseman. In 1900 he joined the 6th Inniskilling Dragoons and served as a subaltern in the Boer War, where he received a serious bullet wound to his left thigh. The injury left him with a shortened leg and was to contribute to his death. On the basis of his skill with horses, Oates was put in charge of the ponies on the *Terra Nova* expedition, though he was not instructed to buy them. He also gave a substantial contribution of £1,000 towards the costs of the expedition, offering his services free. As one of Scott's final South Pole party he suffered particularly badly from malnutrition, frostbite and probably scurvy, affecting his leg wound. He is best remembered for his self-sacrifice in walking out of the tent to his certain death on the return journey on 17 March 1912. He is the only soldier to die in a non-combatant role who is commemorated by the Army.

Omelchenko, Anton Lukisch (1883–1932)

Born in Bat'ki, Russia, Omelchenko was groom on the *Terra Nova* expedition, assisting with the ponies.

Pennell, Harry L. L. (1882–1916)

Pennell was navigator in the *Terra Nova*. A gifted amateur naturalist, he also helped Wilson in the study of birds during the early part of the expedition.

Ponting, Herbert George (1870–1935)

Herbert Ponting was photographer and cinematographer on the *Terra Nova* expedition. Born at Salisbury, Ponting travelled to the United States, after a short interlude in banking, where he worked in ranching and mining before taking up photography in 1900. He travelled widely in the Far East building a reputation for his work.

By 1909 he had an international name as a photographer and was appointed by Scott as 'camera artist' for the *Terra Nova* expedition. Known as 'Ponko' he was inspired by the light and landscape of Antarctica and his black-

and-white work remains unequalled. During the dark winter nights, Ponting entertained the men with lantern-slide shows of his exploits in Japan and China.

As the first professional photographer to visit Antarctica, he created a dramatic and beautiful visual record of the early part of the expedition. Ponting was unable to gain permission from Scott to accompany the Southern Party on their push for the Pole because it was impractical to transport his heavy equipment.

On his return to Britain he released the classic film *90° South* and wrote *The Great White South* (1921) illustrated with many of his photographs.

Royds, Charles W. Rawson (1876–1931)

Born in Rochdale, Charles Royds followed his family tradition and joined the Royal Navy serving initially as a cadet aboard HMS *Conway*. His application to join the *Discovery* expedition was accepted in 1899 and he served as first lieutenant, also making a remarkable journey east across the Ross Ice Shelf to conduct magnetic work. Cape Royds was named after him.

Scott, Captain Robert Falcon (1868–1912)

See chapter 2, (p. 21), chapter 4, (p. 55) and Voyages' End (p. 129).

Shackleton, Sir Ernest Henry (1874–1922)

See chapter 2, (p. 21), chapter 7, (p. 104) and Voyages' End, (p. 129).

Simpson, Dr George Clarke (1878–1965)

Simpson was meteorologist on the *Terra Nova* expedition.

Wild, John Robert Francis (1873–1939)

Known to all as 'Frank', Wild was born in Skelton, North Yorkshire. He spent eleven years in the merchant navy before joining the Royal Navy in 1900. He was chosen from some 3,000 naval applicants to join the *Discovery*. Wild was later selected by Shackleton to serve on the *Nimrod* expedition and was a member of the party to reach the furthest point south at 82°23'. He was leader of the western base party on Douglas Mawson's Australian Antarctic Expedition of 1911–14 aboard the *Aurora*. His brother Ernest Wild, was a member of the ill-fated Ross

Sea Party on the Imperial Trans-Antarctic Expedition, in which three men died.

With such extensive Antarctic experience, and being a warm admirer of Shackleton, he was an automatic choice as second-in-command for the *Endurance* expedition. He remained in command of the men on Elephant Island while they awaited rescue. He went on to sail with Shackleton on his final voyage aboard the *Quest*.

Wilson, Dr Edward Adrian (1872–1912)

Wilson was assistant surgeon on the *Discovery* expedition. A deeply religious man, he was also a skilled artist and his drawings, sketches and paintings present an evocative view of the Antarctic landscape. Wilson's sympathetic character soon marked him out as a key figure in maintaining team spirit and morale. Scott relied heavily on him for advice, guidance and moral support.

He joined the *Terra Nova* as scientific director and zoologist, responsible for the management and welfare of the scientific research team on the expedition. His selfless character earned him the nick-name 'Uncle Bill'. Wilson was automatically a member of the final South Pole party and died alongside Scott and Bowers on the return journey from the Pole.

Worsley, Frank Arthur (1872–1943)

Born at Akaroa, New Zealand, Frank Worsley served as a reserve officer in the Royal Navy, 1904–14, before becoming captain of the *Endurance* in 1914. His navigation and seamanship on the 800-mile voyage of the *James Caird* to South Georgia was outstanding. He served on two ships in World War I and was awarded the DSO and a CBE. He sailed with Shackleton again in the *Quest* in 1921.

Crew Lists

Discovery 1901-1904 – key personnel

Officers:

Robert Falcon Scott, Captain, RN *leader*
Albert B. Armitage, Lieutenant, RNR *navigator and second-in-command*
Michael Barne, Lieutenant RN *magnetician*
Louis C. Bernacchi *physicist*
Hartley T. Ferrar *geologist*
Thomas V. Hodgson *marine biologist*
Reginald Koettlitz *surgeon*
George F. A. Mulock, 2nd Lieutenant, RN
Charles Royds, Lieutenant, RN *meteorologist*
Ernest H. Shackleton, Sub-Lieutenant RNR, third Lt.* *surveyor and photographer*
Reginald Skelton, Lieutenant (E) RN, Chief Engineer*
Edward A. Wilson *assistant surgeon, artist and zoologist*

Warrant Officers (all RN):

Thomas A. Feather, Boatswain
James H. Dellbridge, Second Engineer
Frederick E. Dailey *carpenter*
Charles F. Ford *steward*

Petty Officers (all RN):

Jacob Cross, PO
Edgar Evans, PO
William Smythe, PO
David Allan, PO
Thomas Kennar, PO
William MacFarlane, PO*

Seaman:

Arthur Pilbeam, RN
William L. Heald, RN
James Dell, RN
Frank Wild, RN
Thomas Williamson, RN
George Croucher, RN
Ernest Joyce, RN
Thomas Crean, RN
Jesse Handsley, RN
William J. Weller, MN *dog handler*
William Peters, RN*
John Walker, MN*
James Duncan, MN* *shipwright*
George Vince, RN (died March 1902)
Charles Bonner, RN (died December 1901)

Stokers:

William Lashly, RN
Arthur L. Quartley, RN
Thomas Whitfield, RN
Frank Plumley, RN
William Page, RN*
William Hubert, MN*

Royal Marines:

Arthur Blissett, lance corporal
Gilbert Scott, private

Civilians:

Henry Brett* *cook*
Charles Clarke *cook*
Clarence Hare* *assistant steward*
Horace Buckridge* *laboratory assistant*

* The list is taken from Scott's *Voyage of the Discovery*; added to it are the men who spent only one Antarctic winter with the expedition, marked with an asterisk, who – with the exception of Shackleton and Mulock – were not listed in the book. Clarke took over duties of cook from Brett.

Nimrod 1907-09 – key personnel

Ernest H. Shackleton *leader*
T.W. Edgeworth David *chief scientist*
Jameson Boyd-Adams *meteorologist*
Philip Brocklehurst *assistant geologist and surveyor*
Bernard Day *motor specialist*
Ernest Joyce *in charge of dogs, sledges and equipment*
Alistair Mackay *surgeon and biologist*
Douglas Mawson *physicist*

Bertram Armytage *in charge of ponies*
Eric Marshall *surgeon and cartographer*
George Marston *artist*
James Murray-Levick *biologist*
Raymond Priestley *geologist*
William Cook *cook*
Frank Wild *in charge of stores*

Terra Nova 1910-13 – key personnel

Robert Falcon Scott, Captain, CVO, RN *leader*
George P. Abbot, PO, RN
W. W. Archer, late RN, Chief Steward
Edward L. Atkinson, RN, Surgeon and Parisitologist
Henry R. Bowers, Lieutenant, RIM
Frank V. Browning, PO, 2nd class, RN
Wilfrid M. Bruce, Lieutenant, RN
Victor L.A. Campbell, Lieutenant, RN
Thomas Clissold, late RN *cook*
Thomas Crean, PO, RN
Apsley Cherry-Garrard *assistant zoologist*
Bernard C. Day *motor specialist*
Frank Debenham *geologist*
Henry Dickason, AB, RN
Francis R. H. Drake, Assistant Paymaster, RN
Edgar Evans, PO, RN
Edward R.G.R. Evans, Lieutenant, RN
Robert Forde, PO, RN
Dimitri Gerov *dog driver*

Tryggve Gran, Sub-Lieutenant, Norwegian *ski expert*
F.J. Hooper, late RN *steward*
W. Lashly, Chief Stoker
G. Murray Levick, RN, Surgeon
Dennis G. Lillie *biologist*
Cecil H. Meares *in charge of dog teams*
Lawrence E.G. Oates, Captain, 6th Inns Dragoons
Anton Omelchenko *groom*
Harry L. L. Pennell, Lieutenant, RN
Herbert G. Ponting *camera artist*
Raymond E. Priestley *geologist*
Edward W. Nelson *biologist*
Henry F. de P. Rennick, Lieutenant, RN
George C. Simpson *meteorologist*
T. Griffith Taylor *geologist*
Thomas S. Williamson, PO, RN
Edward A. Wilson *chief of the scientific staff and zoologist*
Charles S. Wright *physicist*

Endurance 1914-16 – key personnel

Ernest H. Shackleton *leader*
William Bakewell, Seaman
Percy Blackborrow *stowaway – later steward*
Alfred Cheetham, Third Officer
Robert Clark *biologist*
Thomas Crean, Second Officer
Charles Green *cook*
Lionel Greenstreet, First Officer
Ernest Holness *fireman*
Walter How, Seaman
Hubert Hudson, Second Officer
Frank Hurley *camera artist*
Leonard Hussey *meteorologist*
Reginald James *physicist*

Alfred Kerr, Second engineer
Timothy McCarthy, Seaman
James McIlroy *surgeon*
Thomas McLeod, Seaman
Henry McNeish *carpenter*
Alexander Macklin, Chief Surgeon
George Marston *artist*
Thomas Orde-Lees *ski expert and store keeper*
Louis Rickinson, Chief Engineer
William Stephenson, Stoker
John Vincent, Boatswain
Frank Wild, Second-in-Command
James Wordie *geologist*
Frank Worsley, Captain

Bibliography and suggested further reading

Alexander, Caroline, *The Endurance: Shackleton's Legendary Antarctic Expedition* (1999)

Amundsen, Roald, *Sydpolen (The South Pole)* (1912)

Arnold, H.J.P., *Photographer of the World: the Biography of Herbert Ponting* (1969)

Bainbridge, Beryl, *The Birthday Boys* (1991)

Barnes, John, *Pioneers of the British Film* (1988)

Bickel, Lennard, *In Search of Frank Hurley* (1980)

Bickel, Lennard, *Shackleton's Forgotten Men* (2000)

Borchgrevink, C.E., *First on the Antarctic Continent* (1901)

Brownlow, Kevin, *The War, the West and the Wilderness* (1978)

Cherry-Garrard, Apsley, *The Worst Journey in the World* (1922)

Feeney, Robert E., *Polar Journeys: the role of food and nutrition in early exploration* (1997)

Fiennes, Sir Ranulph, *To the Ends of the Earth* (1983)

Fiennes, Sir Ranulph, *Mind over Matter* (1993)

Foreign and Commonwealth Office/British Antarctic Survey, *Antarctica (Schools Pack)* (1999)

Fuchs, Sir Vivian and Hillary, Sir Edmund, *The Crossing of Antarctica* (1958)

Fuchs, Sir Vivian, *Of Ice and Men* (1982)

Fuchs, Sir Vivian, *A Time to Speak* (1990)

Gran, Tryggve, *The Norwegian with Scott* (1984)

Hempleman-Adams, David *Toughing it Out* (1997)

Hempleman-Adams, David, *Walking on Thin Ice* (1998)

Huntford, Roland, *The Amundsen Photographs* (1987)

Huntford, Roland, *Scott and Amundsen* [republished as *The Last Place on Earth*] (1979)

Huntford, Roland, *Shackleton* (1985)

Hurley, Frank, *Argonauts of the South* (1925)

Huxley, Elspeth, *Scott of the Antarctic* (1977)

Limb, S. and Cordingley, P., *Captain Oates: Soldier and Explorer* (1982)

Locke, Stephen, *George Marston: Shackleton's Antarctic Artist* (2000)

Lowell, Thomas, *Sir Hubert Wilkins: His World of Adventure* (1961)

Mawson, Sir Douglas, *The Home of the Blizzard* (1915)

Mills, Leif, *Frank Wild* (1999)

Ponting, Herbert, *The Great White South* (1921)

Preston, Diana, *A First Rate Tragedy: Captain Scott's Antarctic Expeditions* (1997)

Riffenburgh, Beau and Cruwys, Liz, *The Photographs of H.G. Ponting* (1998)

Savours, Ann, *Scott's Last Voyage: through the Antarctic Camera of Herbert Ponting* (1974)

Savours, Ann, *The Voyages of the Discovery: The Illustrated History of Scott's Ship* (1992)

Scott, R.F., *The Voyage of the Discovery* (1905)

Scott, R. F., (ed. Huxley, Leonard), *Scott's Last Expedition* (1913)

Shackleton, Sir Ernest, *Aurora Australis* (1908)

Shackleton, Sir Ernest, *The Heart of the Antarctic* (1909)

Shackleton, Sir Ernest, *South* (1919)

Spufford, Francis, *I may be some time: Ice and the English Imagination* (1996)

Stroud, Mike, *Shadows on the Wasteland* (1993)

Wheeler, Sarah, *Terra Incognita* (1996)

Wilson, E.A., (ed. Savours, Ann), *The Diary of the Discovery Expedition to the Antarctic Regions (1901-1904)* (1966)

Worsley, Frank A., *Shackleton's Boat Journey* (1940)

Recommended Websites

Catalogued reviews of these and other websites can be located in PORT,
the National Maritime Museum's maritime information gateway, http://www.port.nmm.ac.uk

Antarctic Co-operative Research Centre, http://www.antcrc.utas.edu.au/antcrc/
Antarctic Philately, http://www.south-pole.com/
Antarctica New Zealand, http://www.antarcticanz.govt.nz/
Australian Antarctic Division, http://www.antdiv.gov.au/
Automated Astrophysical Site-Testing Observatory webcam, http://bat.phys.unsw.edu.au/~aasto/
British Antarctic Survey, http://www.antarctica.ac.uk/
Byrd Polar Research Center, http://www-brpc.mps.ohio-state.edu/
Cheltenham Art Gallery and Museum, http://www.cheltenham.gov.uk/agm/Sites/AGM.htm
Council of Managers of National Antarctic Programs, http://www.comnap.aq
Discovery Point, http://www.rrs-discovery.co.uk/
Edinburgh University Library, http://www.lib.ed.ac.uk/
EELS, http://eels.lub.lu.se/
Endurance, http://www.kodak.com/US/en/corp/features/endurance/
GLACIER, http://www.glacier.rice.edu/
Heritage America, http://www.heritage-antarctica.org/
Journal for Maritime Research, http://www.jmr.nmm.ac.uk/
National Library of Scotland, http://www.nls.ac.uk/
National Maritime Museum, Greenwich, London, http://www.nmm.ac.uk/
NMM Search Station, http://www.nmm.ac.uk/searchstation/
Natural Environment Research Council, http://www.nerc.ac.uk
Norwegian Explorers, http://www.odin.dep.no/ud/nonytt/uda-299.html
Norwegian Polar Institute, http://www.npolar.no/
Office of Polar Programs at the National Science Foundation, http://www.nsf.gov/od/opp/
Royal Geographic Society, http://www.rgs.org/
Scientific Committee on Antarctic Research, http://www.scar.org/
Scott Polar Research Institute, University of Cambridge, http://www.spri.cam.ac.uk
Shackleton's Antarctic Odyssey, http://www.pbs.org/wgbh/nova/shackleton/

Index